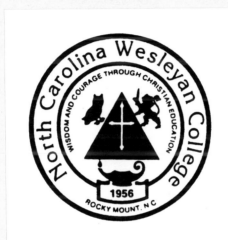

THEOLOGY AND THE CHURCH

A Response to Cardinal Ratzinger and a Warning to the Whole Church

REVISED EDITION

Juan Luis Segundo, S.J.

Translated by John W. Diercksmeier

1817

Harper & Row, Publishers, San Francisco

idge, Hagerstown, New York, Philadelphia, Washington
ondon, Mexico City, São Paulo, Singapore, Sydney

To the two persons to whom I owe my life, and the two things that make it human: a sense of humor and affection. To my father and my mother, then, this book is written with humor and affection—although to others it may not appear so.

FIRST HARPER & ROW PAPERBACK EDITION PUBLISHED IN 1987.

Library of Congress Cataloging-in-Publication Data

Segundo, Juan Luis.
    Theology and the Church.

    Translated from the Spanish.
    Reprint. Originally published: Minneapolis : Winston Press ; London : G. Chapman, c1985.
    1. Catholic Church.   Congregatio pro Doctrina Fidei. Instructio de quibusdam rationibus "theologiae liberationibus."   2. Liberation theology—Controversial   literature.   3. Catholic Church—Doctrines.   4. Ratzinger, Joseph.   I. Title.
BT83.57.C375 1984 Suppl. 2   230'.2   87-400
ISBN 0-06-254704-6 (pbk.)

87 88 89 90 91 MPC 10 9 8 7 6 5 4 3 2 1

CONTENTS

1

THE KEY
TO READING THIS BOOK

The title of this chapter is not pretentious, although it may seem so to some readers. Its only purpose is to alert the reader to the fact that (contrary to what usually happens with prologues, prefaces, and introductions) this chapter should *not* be skipped over—at least if the reader is truly interested in what follows.

Preparing the Reader

What was feared in Latin America a few years ago has taken place. Six years ago, the Puebla Conference met in a cautious atmosphere: everything seemed to indicate that its participants were preparing a condemnation of that theological current which in Latin America was called the theology of liberation.

However, that did not happen at Puebla. A compromise document emerged from the Third General Conference of Latin American Bishops. But today, a new reading of that document—in light of the *Instruction on the Theology of Liberation* which was published by the Vatican's Congregation for the Doctrine of the Faith on August 6, 1984—will show that the principal elements for its condemnation were already present in the Puebla document.

Puebla did not, however, bring those elements together and arrive at the conclusion to which they pointed—at least not the sensational conclusion that the international press avidly awaited. This was due to the undeniable influence of a group of bishops, aided by an important group of theologians, who worked toward a consensus and who did not cease (even outside the hall) to play a most important role in the discussion. Thus, the result was that every critical element was accompanied by another—distinct rather than opposed—that nuanced it and therefore prevented it from being one-sided.

The relief at the finally approved text—in spite of the corrections introduced by the Roman Curia after the closing of the Puebla Conference—was immense. No clear condemnation arose from the Conference. The press, expecting a sensational statement, could not and did not know how to read it as they had wanted to. In the Christian world there were those who thought that the danger had been contrived. Among "liberation" theologians, many expressed a kind of triumphalism. Ignoring here and abridging there, they wrote books and taught courses about Puebla, presenting the long episcopal document as a reaffirmation of Vatican II and of the Second General Conference of Latin American Bishops at Medellín. "Medellín and Puebla" today constitutes a formula as overused as it is mistaken, in the sense that we cannot cite the two documents as belonging to the same line of theology.

It is not strange then that what was impossible within Latin America was accomplished in Rome and elsewhere. That was to be expected—without the active presence and general consultation of the Latin American bishops, and without the need to compromise so that reactionaries mixed opposing statements in a shadow world where all cats are viewed as leopards. It was then possible for the forces of reaction to devote all their strength and vigor to arguments against the theology of liberation and thus arrive at the logical consequences of the adduced principles: that, speaking in general, liberation theology proposes "a novel interpretation of both the content of faith and of Christian existence which seriously departs from the faith of the Church and, in fact, actually constitutes a practical negation" (VI,9).

Except for the pain that a statement such as this will always cause, it is good that this finally has been said blatantly since it allows people to know where they stand without being caught in verbal shadow-boxing or in vague and unspecified attacks.

But before considering the scope and particular elements of this apparently radical condemnation, one must return to a fact that will be very important for the interpretation of this document.

Several months before the appearance of the document, there was a rumor that the Congregation of the Faith, headed by Cardinal Ratzinger, was preparing a statement attacking the theology of liberation. Furthermore, there appeared a critical and somewhat strange article, published by Cardinal Ratzinger himself in an Italian journal, directed at the Latin American theology of liberation.

The odd thing about this article is that the Cardinal did not seem to have any direct information about the theology in question. The article differed (as would be seen later) from the document being prepared in that the latter demonstrated a fairly precise knowledge (although one may argue about perspective and depth) of Latin American theology.

Cardinal Ratzinger's article seemed to come from a European who reads European phenomena and tendencies into a non-European context. As an example, he speaks of the supposed influence of Rudolf Bultmann on liberation theology. Of course, one cannot presume that the Latin American liberation theologians, having been educated in Europe, would be unfamiliar with Bultmann or even that they may be more immune than any European theologian to the impact of one of the most influential theologians of this century. However, insofar as those liberation theologians are integrated into the Latin American context, there is nothing further from that context than the Bultmannian methodology and agenda. One needs only to think of "demythologization," born of the "death of God" and proper to the "developed" mentality of the modern world; the rejection of the search for the historical Jesus and of the historical causes of his death; the purely eschatological, ahistorical idea of the coming of the kingdom of God supposedly preached by Jesus; the method of personalistic, existential biblical interpretation, without any depth or social analysis; and so on.

The reason Cardinal Ratzinger's article is mentioned here is that it contributed—in an atmosphere where from one day to the next a condemnation from the Congregation for the Doctrine of the Faith was expected—to the creation of a common (and one might even say understandable) psychological defense mechanism. After the appearance of Cardinal Ratzinger's article, there was the supposition that, under the title of "the theology of liberation," the condemnation would be of a deformation, a caricature, in which *no serious theologian in Latin America would be recognized.*

It was assumed that the theologian who takes this position would be seeking, beforehand and in bad faith, some kind of escape clause, and it was equally assumed that this attitude is the same as denying proper submission to the magisterium of the Church. It is interesting to note that the document itself refers to the difficulty of dialogue with Latin American theologians (see X,3) and of even questioning them. Before responding to this, and in order to do so, it is necessary to note a few points.

Recently there has been much discussion about the functions and scope of the magisterium on the one hand, and of theological investigation and publication on the other. I have always maintained that it is not my intention to enter into this polemic, where a consensus satisfactory to both parties is far from being achieved.

Because the reader has the right to know on what level my commentary moves, I will try to summarize succinctly the basic norms that govern these pages. Let us begin by establishing a fundamental fact: the document we are analyzing does not belong to the extraordinary magisterium but to the *ordinary*. The extraordinary magisterium would have been involved if the document had been the result of an ecumenical council that intended to establish questions of faith or morals, or if it were the result of an *ex cathedra* statement by a Roman Pontiff upon these questions. This is apart from the issue as to how a written formula belonging to the extraordinary magisterium should be understood and what limits it may have. In any case, it is a tenet of Roman Catholic faith that such a magisterium is infallible.

On the contrary, and with the same universality, it is understood that the ordinary magisterium of the Church, despite the respect it deserves and the sincere obedience it demands, is *fallible*. In other words, it is subject to error. Two important truths are equally admitted and so must be treated here.

The *first* is that this possibility of error must not be considered as merely hypothetical. The hypocrisy of "forgetting" its fallibility would not show respect for the magisterium but rather a lack of respect toward the magisterium *in its essence*—which is, to teach. As Cardinal Lercaro said, this is the case, not in spite of our love for the truth but precisely because of our love for it. And we know that (normally) to fall into error and correct it is a deeper path toward a truth than one which is obtained through the mere repetition of past teaching.

But there is also the daily reality of the perplexity engendered in every Christian by the ordinary magisterium's fallibility. Its function, as has already been stated, is one of teaching and orientation, proper to the bishops as representatives of the apostolicity of the Church, either gathered in synods or conferences or acting individually in their own dioceses. And everyone in the Church is aware to what extent the teachings or orientations of the bishops are often different when one crosses the borders of a particular diocese or bishops' conference.

However, what is of more interest here is that the magisterium which the Supreme Pontiffs themselves have exercised most often is itself the ordinary magisterium (discourses, encyclicals, documents of pontifical commissions) and is therefore equally fallible. It would be very naive to think that, because a papal encyclical cites a few "predecessors of happy memory," one must conclude that all popes follow a single line of theology. Moreover, every theologian worthy of the name can cite cases in which the mere fallibility of this magisterium became an actual error. There are cases, some of them very well known and painful, which have caused grave damage to the Church until reflection by the faithful—on all levels—succeeded in correcting them.

For instance, the famous *Syllabus* of Pope Pius IX condemned the opinion of those who say that "in our day it is no longer necessary to consider the Catholic religion as the only state religion, excluding all others" (Denzniger, 1777-78), but this itself was later condemned as theologically false. This condemnation of religious freedom, made by the ordinary magisterium of a Supreme Pontiff, was in effect for a whole century (one century and one year, to be exact: 1864-1965). In order to go *passively* from error to truth, one had to wait for Vatican II to declare solemnly that "the human person has a right to religious liberty" and that "this right . . . must be given recognition in the constitutional order of society" (*Dignitatis humanae*, 2). I said "passively," because not everyone, thanks be to God, was resigned to wait for this to be said. I would like to remind the reader—who today lives peacefully in the security that the Church has for some time (if not always) defended human rights (among them the right of religious freedom)—that during the century from the *Syllabus* to Vatican II, the first theologian (it always starts with one) who publicly defended what today is commonly accepted had dared, *for love of the Church*, to challenge the weight of a structure which condemned his thought. This is not meant as an excuse for dissidence; but neither should it be forgotten.

The *second* truth is that this possibility of error cannot be an excuse for minimizing either the respect due the ordinary magisterium or the obligation of obeying it when it exercises its function of teaching. Obviously this obligation, like all those of an educational nature, is not blind, nor does it lead to a blind will and passive submission. It is not relativist nor pragmatic. It does not suppose, for example, that the entire Church is going to pass, overnight and magically, from condemnation to defense of the freedom of worship.

As in every educational process—and the process of faith certainly is educational—the responsibilities of searching, of freedom, and of criticism grow insofar as the reasons which move the ordinary magisterium of the Church to take a particular position are better understood and appreciated. And conversely, the obligation to accept a particular solution or teaching grows insofar as one does not have even the elements needed to understand and judge it in perspective, whether because of a lack of education or of maturity.

Between these two poles, creativity on the one hand and due submission on the other, there are no easy or univocal solutions. The balance is difficult, demanding, and often poses painful qualms of conscience. It should be noted that it is difficult and demanding not only for Christians with regard to the magisterium, but also for the magisterium with regard to all Christians. We might add that, besides being difficult and demanding, it is painful for both parties.

Moreover, this difficulty has increased in recent times. We should be happy about this, at least because the growing difficulty stems from the Christian layperson's taking, seriously and responsibly, the obligation pointed out by the Council. The layperson is not to be a merely passive recipient of the formulas of faith but a person who uses them to seek the most human solution to the problems that arise in history (*Gaudium et Spes*, 11). The laity are not to think that the ecclesiastical hierarchy—the bishops and priests, the ordinary magisterium—has as its mission or possibility to give prefabricated answers (*Gaudium et Spes*, 43). It is obvious that the role of the laity does not abolish the function of the magisterium but rather introduces (or should introduce) important changes in that function.

Now, if there are no magical solutions for the problems this causes, the question that arises is especially painful for those who, in some way, have a foot in each camp, or rather, for those who have a role in both of the functions which should be integrated in this elusive synthesis.

I am referring to the *theologian*. The document analyzed here (like the events that, more or less simultaneously, have attracted the media) does not point to the laity, at least not directly, but to a particular "theology"; that is, in more personal terms, to the group of theologians who support it. It is only from that dogmatic consideration that one then arrives at pastoral action and, from there, at the faith of the laity.

As a result, it may be the theological function, more than that of the magisterium or of the laity (the two extremes), which must confront what is primarily divisive when it should be a synthesis. Responsible to both the magisterium and the laity, the theologian theoretically *knows* that the two loyalties should be the single loyalty to Jesus Christ, whose Spirit acts in the magisterium as well as in the laity (although in different ways). But the theologian does not always *perceive* how precisely to bring them together, especially when dealing with the ordinary magisterium, or rather, with a function that may err and that has erred, but which cannot therefore be minimized or cast aside.

The aforementioned attitude must be understood in this context of the theologian's double loyalty, both fundamental and often painful—an attitude assumed by many theologians preceding the publication of a document which was rumored to contain a negative judgment about the theology of liberation.

However, it is not possible to argue, from everything that has been said, that the correct attitude would have been to examine the magisterium's decision with a dispassionate or indifferent expectation. Theology is not so frivolous nor does the effort to understand one's own faith and the faith of others remain so negligible as to permit one to methodically ignore what has been for so many years the object of profound search on the part of theologians.

Nor is the correct attitude reduced to vigorously opposing beforehand strong negative feelings toward the observations, corrections, or warnings that might come from the magisterium. However, one always hopes that theological investigation and the shared praxis which stems from it will pass through the filter of what, is some way, is condemned.

There is another reason why this attitude should not seem strange. Examined closely, to condemn (or even to make observations or pertinent corrections) means first of all to describe what is being judged. And it is no easy matter to give an exact description of something that may have been expressed over a long period of time, often with specific nuances in a single or several works. Therefore, in all good faith and often not without valid reasons, the author or authors to whom the condemnation points do not see themselves as being included in it. Sometimes the very need to be direct and clear as to what is being condemned leads (unconsciously, it is supposed) to simplifying or avoiding important elements or nuances.

There are, as the whole theological world knows, many and even celebrated examples; I want to cite a single though certainly important one. In the *Revue des Sciences Philosophiques et Théologiques* (1984, 68:2, p.277), there is a long review of an author of the importance of Yves Congar in Edmund Schlink's *Ecumenical Dogmatics*. It says: "S[chlink] compares the statements of the Council of Trent with those of the Confessions of Augsburg. He notes, *rightly,* that *the canons of Trent do not apply to Luther*." Magnificent! But it took four centuries to discover that the "description" of what was condemned was not faithful to the original!

In a more modest and infinitely less serious case than that of the Reformation, the theology of liberation has been accustomed for many years to being attacked in a manner that is almost a caricature. What has awakened deep anger and division was not an a priori negative criticism of its possible value and orthodoxy—and still less so if the gospel is taken into account. But it is true that in the heat of battle, among those who would defend liberation theology as well as those who would attack it, extreme positions, or at least ones that are imbalanced and insufficiently nuanced, are sometimes taken.

We already knew, in theory and through experience, that a theology that has been spread, carried out in practice, used and reused, and accommodated to theoretical and practical concerns is defenseless against what we might call the "termite technique." With the aid of conference minutes, mimeographed texts, and citations from less-representative theologians, it is always possible to create a convincing picture of what one is trying to criticize. If to this we add taking quotations out of context and even (it happens) citing critiques that the liberation theologians must themselves make from time to time (out of sincerity and love for the truth) of particular excesses or simplifications, one will always have a deformed picture (of any theology) that can justify any criticism. This may even lead the unwary to condemn other trends—very different in value— simply because they use vaguely similar terms or expressions.[1]

Certainly there was no fear that a Roman Congregation could arrive at such an extreme. A certain measure of ill will would have been necessary. But in an excessively wide context where limits were impossible to fix, everything depended (at least so we thought before seeing the document) on how it would "define" or "describe" critically what it understood by liberation theology. In other words, everything depends on the "expressions," "positions," or "productions" (terms used by the document) utilized for a judgment which (we knew then) would be negative.

The Document Itself

At the beginning of September 1984, the *Instruction on Certain Aspects of the "Theology of Liberation,"*—dated August 6, 1984, and signed by Cardinal Ratzinger, Prefect of the Congregation for the Doctrine of the Faith—was published in the media.

How was the document received, especially by those to whom it pointed, the Latin American liberation theologians? I cannot know for certain. I cannot show any statistics and, furthermore, I doubt that they would have much value, at least not for me.

However, I do believe a rudimentary (certainly a very simple) typology is possible within which there can be countless variations. I am not trying here to judge my colleagues but rather to illuminate my own position.

As I have already said, it is possible, in principle, to reduce the impact of the *Instruction* by limiting its reach. One might look for that at the limitations that the document itself admits explicitly. One can also restrict its impact by showing that, while the document does not limit itself to such-and-such forms of liberation theology, its criticism (precisely because it could seem an exaggeration and a caricature) points (without saying so) only to *certain* expressions or positions of that theology—and not to that entire theology itself. If neither of these two restrictions were to apply, it would then be necessary to affirm that the *Instruction* attacks, and even condemns, *all* forms of liberation theology, no matter how serious, balanced, or well-founded they may appear to their authors. In such a case, it would remain for these theologians, logically, to choose between honoring what the *Instruction* sustains and introducing the necessary corrections, or showing, respectfully but firmly, why they think this document of the ordinary magisterium is mistaken.

Perhaps the closeness to the complex and inhuman situation which the Latin American people so visibly suffer has at this time induced a large part of the hierarchy (upon whom the Latin American theologians depend) to view the document as no condemnation of *all* theologies of liberation.[2] Currently this seems to be a fairly general tendency; contrary to the mass media, the hierarchy has been mostly silent about the document. In some instances, the interpretation given to the Vatican document, such as the one represented by the Superior General of the Society of Jesus, who is very close to its sources, is that the *Instruction* "apostolically purifies by clarifying the argumentation of *some* theologians of liberation" (Statement by Very Reverend Peter-Hans Kolvenbach, S.J., dated September 3, 1984).

It is logical to think, I believe, that this "some"—this limitation of scope—must result from an awareness of the explicit intentions of the document. It would not appear that Father Kolvenbach sees a need to so limit the document because of caricatures or excessive generalizations within it.

It is true that the document carries in its very title the significant restriction of referring to "certain aspects" of liberation theology. It admits, further, that from a common nucleus—"a special concern for the poor and the victims of oppression, which in turn begets a commitment to justice"—there may derive many opinions and "we can distinguish *several*, often contradictory *ways* of understanding the Christian meaning of poverty and the type of commitment to justice which it requires." These "diverse theological positions" justify the use often made throughout the *Instruction* of the plural "theologies of liberation" (III,3; cf. VI,8).

Now then, it is true that one of the two paragraphs which most clearly expresses the intention of the document limits it to criticism of "the deviations, and risks of deviation, damaging to the faith and to Christian living, that are brought about by certain forms of liberation theology" (Introduction). The second presents a similar limitation. *After speaking of the pluralism of liberation theologies*, it states "in this present document, we will only be discussing developments of that current of thought which is called 'theology of liberation,' and proposes a novel interpretation of both the content of faith and of Christian existence which seriously departs from the faith of the Church and, in fact, actually constitutes a practical negation" (VI,9). The difficulty lies in not knowing what is limited by the adverb "only" because it is misplaced in the sentence. It can mean that the author will discuss either (a) developments of liberation theology *instead of* other possible subjects, or (b) everything that falls under the subject of "liberation theology" *but not* other theologies; or (c) those particular expressions of liberation theology that may be a practical negation of faith because they present a new conception of faith and Christian existence *but not* those expressions of liberation theology that do not have this negative (if that is what it is) character.

An indication that this latter reductive interpretation has prevailed is the relative silence and calm (even indifference) with which the *Instruction* has sometimes been received, even though it says, at the very least, that certain forms of liberation theology depart from the faith of the Church. It would seem that the Catholic hierarchy in Latin America does not give so general a scope to the *Instruction* as to be urged to investigate and attack what has been condemned—the alleged practical negation of Christian faith. Implicitly the hierarchy seems to consider those "results" as something very exceptional.

Be that as it may, the explicit limitations set by the *Instruction* itself have provided a basis on which some Latin American theologians have already declared that the *Instruction* does not affect them. This is not because of pride but because they do not see their thought reflected in those "certain aspects" which are condemned. I may or may not be forgiven for pointing out that I believe this to be false confidence on their part.

For, I am not sure that the explicit intention of the Vatican document admits such facile reductions in its scope. Without denying that they are present *in principle*, I believe that the document points to something it considers to be almost universal when it refers to liberation theology, or when it uses the plural without the simple restriction of "certain" or "some." It is true that the document states (always in principle and although this principle may be very vague) that "in itself, the expression 'theology of liberation' is a thoroughly valid term" (III,4; see Introduction; III,2; VI,5).

Yet that very general principle, falling under the discernment of faith and of the magisterium, seems to cover nothing more than the generic aspiration of the liberation of the oppressed and (also very generic) a "preferential option for the poor." On the other hand, it associates practically inevitable negative elements with that commitment. These are lumped together with the "deviations" and with the "risks of deviation"; and it states that these risks, in spite of being only risks, are already *"damaging to the faith."* It states that the "pathos" or passion with which that commitment is lived is the cause of "the aspiration for justice [which] often finds itself the captive of ideologies" (II,3). "The different theologies of liberation" are all exposed to the "temptation to reduce the Gospel to an earthly gospel" (VI,5). "It is not uncommon" for ideological aspects to be predominant among "the 'theologians of liberation'" (VII,6). It

finally states that "the positions here in question are often brought
out explicitly in certain of the writings of 'theologians of liberation.'
In others, they follow logically from their premises. . . . This
[Christian] message in its entirety finds itself then called into question by the 'theologies of liberation'" (IX,1).

Consequently, the *Instruction*, above all beginning with Chapter
VII, widely uses the simple plural "theologies of liberation," *without
any apparent limitation*, to indicate the collective subject to which it
attributes the more serious deviations, or rather, those "positions
which are incompatible with the Christian vision of humanity"
(VIII,1).

It is true that in the final "Orientations" it speaks again of the
"serious deviations of some 'theologies of liberation'" (XI,1). But
then it returns to the simple and limitless plural to say nothing less
than that "the 'theologies of liberation' especially tend to misunderstand or to eliminate" essential aspects such as "the transcendence
and gratuity of liberation in Jesus Christ, . . . the sovereignty of
grace, and the true nature of the means of salvation, especially of the
Church and the sacraments" (XI,17).

Utilizing the simple plural when just as easily, in matters of such
seriousness, it could have been limited with a single word, "some" or
"certain", shows that the document consciously goes beyond the
mere denunciation of particular, rare, or peripheral excesses.[3] I
believe that this constitutes a true hermeneutical principle if one is
to correctly read the entire *Instruction* as well as each of its
paragraphs.

One of my Latin American colleagues, in a memorandum on the
Vatican document and its proper interpretation, writes what I am
here summarizing: "I adhere loyally and in responsible obedience
to the pastoral "Orientations" with which the document ends
(XI). . . . With even greater reason, I unreservedly adhere to *the
doctrinal judgments upon the faith* contained in the body of the
document. . . . I also adhere to *the great anthropological, social,
and ethical-political principles* that the document reaffirms. . . .
But, out of ecclesial loyalty, I must give witness to the fact that *I do
not know* . . . theologians *in Latin America* who support the
'reductive' interpretations of the faith described by the document or

who deny those great principles of the Christian conception of humanity and society" (my colleague's emphasis).

This statement establishes, if I am not mistaken, three things: (a) the theological principles, and the theological and humanistic conclusions drawn from them, are perfectly acceptable; (b) in terms of the dogmatic "facts" to which it refers, the application of those principles to any reality known by the theologian is false; and (c) the Latin American theologian who makes this statement is not affected by the principles (which he accepts) or by the description of the facts (which he rejects).

I believe that to understand and appreciate the true value of this type of statement (where a person defends his or her most basic loyalties) is to fail to remember something that has already been stated here. The Vatican document poses a serious and painful question of conscience, above all for theologians committed to pastoral activity— which is the same as saying, committed to the living problems of those whom they serve. It is only by remembering that context and making an effort to place oneself within it that one can ascertain the sincerity which each response contains. What better criterion of that sincerity than the price paid for it?

Therefore, I do not question the personal sincerity of such a response. Moreover, it awakens my sympathy and appeals to my sense of solidarity. Nevertheless, I must say that an interpretation made within those parameters or leading to those conclusions, though it is sincere, does not recognize the Vatican document as the serious thrust it constitutes.

I do not expect to be believed without proof, which will be given in the next chapter. But I believe it worthwhile to state here how I approach the *Instruction* on liberation theology.

First, I want to make clear that I am profoundly affected by it. Let me be clear: I understand that my theology (that is, my interpretation of Christian faith) is false if the theology of the document is true—or if it is the only true one.

I do not deny that there are elements of caricature in the *Instruction's* description of some traits of liberation theology. I deny, hence, that all its criticisms may be equally valid. When, for example, it speaks of "concepts uncritically [or not sufficiently critically] borrowed from Marxist ideology" (VI,10), I am not affected by that criticism because, instead of observing certain common grounds upon which one may or may not accept what stems from that ideology, I have written, among other things, an entire volume, *Faith and Ideologies*, containing precisely that "careful epistemological critique." Under those conditions, I believe that it would only be foolish to say that, in this case, "impatience and a desire for results" had led me "to turn to . . . Marxist analysis" (VII,1). Yet, as I have already pointed out, I do not think that the existence in the document of certain caricatures can become a universal escape hatch.

Second I say this because the document goes beyond that possible limitation. And it does this although the attempt to place all "liberation theology'' under a negative theological judgment means for the *Instruction* to have to pay a very high price. And that price has a lot to do with honesty.

Let me explain. From the moment that one intends to expound a negative evaluation of an entire theological current—showing that its "deviations and risks of deviation,"[4] lead to a "practical negation of Christian faith,"—two paths are open.

One is the old path of exhibiting quotations of theological propositions to show how the thought that arises from them departs from the Christian faith and even negates it (although it may be only in its practical consequences). This path has advantages but also one clear disadvantage. (I am referring here, of course, to advantages or disadvantages for the persons composing the document.) The advantage is that the argument is so simple—there is really no need for many examples. The mere fact of citing written statements discharges one from proving the fact. And the mere comparison of the quotation with the common theological consensus is enough to justify the condemnation. But the disadvantage is equally great, above all when dealing with a current of thought that has widely different manifestations: the quotation loses in *extension* what it gains (for the condemnation) in precision.

It is easy to argue that the quoted expressions do not represent the *entire* thought of the theologian, who may have others that correct or complement those expressions. Or it may be that such expressions are only found in theologians who sustain extreme, unbalanced, or unnuanced positions. In a word, one can argue against the condemnation—founded upon quotations—of an entire current of thought on the ground that only the "caricature" is condemned. Consequently, such defects (it is presumed) will not be found in the better and more serious representatives of the thought in question.

The other path is that of attacking the tendency *as such*. In that case it becomes very difficult to take hold of specific quotations. Everything must be taken as an organic whole together and must, even more so, reject the deformed and the unbalanced in order to arrive at its genuine core. There is still the need—in dealing with theological currents practiced within the Church as part of its daily life—to show what important elements (which in themselves or at first sight do not shock) are unacceptable in a healthy theology. The advantage of this second path is that one attacks something which is common and basic to all the expressions of a particular theology—in this case the theology of liberation as such. And this is, from my perspective, the more honest path that the Vatican Congregation for the Doctrine of the Faith follows—at least in this case.

The disadvantage of this path is, however, greater than is commonly thought. I refer to the price that must be paid so that the condemnation may touch generally and effectively upon the entire current in question. Contrary to the quotation method mentioned above, this latter method must before all else resist the temptation of simplistic, schematic, or tendentious descriptions—as has already been stated. On the other hand, if one does not use such descriptions in the case of a theology already widely practiced and accepted in the Church, one needs to take up a much more detailed and explicit argument. It is not enough to appeal to either common sense or Christian tradition; one must counter one argument with another, one theology with another theology. And thus everybody would be able to discover the very theology on which the condemnation is based.

This is very important, and all the more so because common language has accepted as very natural the opposition between particular "theologians" on the one hand and the "magisterium" on the other. It would seem as if the former argued simply from theology while the latter argued from faith. This is not so. Without denying institutional differences, the magisterium also has its theology. By definition, no one can explain faith and define its limits without understanding it, that is, without a definite theology.

This is not said as if it were a novel interpretation destined to relativize or detract from the magisterium. Within the pluralism that will always be necessary for the people who make up the Church to continue seeking the truth (which is always greater than what is presently possessed), the magisterium can and must point out cases in which a theology does not fall within the healthy variety of thought that the Church both needs and accepts. To fulfill the task of teaching to which the word "magisterium" itself points, one must condemn not just a name but an interpretation: what is coherent with faith must be opposed to what is not. Speaking of the ordinary magisterium, furthermore, one sees all the more clearly that its permanent and ongoing magisterial function will be much better served the more it can explain, with the support of sound theological reasoning, why it must exclude a certain current of theological thought from the existing pluralism.

There is a well-known example related to this subject. Two weeks before his death, Karl Rahner wrote to the Cardinal Archbishop of Lima and proclaimed, "I am convinced of the orthodoxy of the theological work of Gustavo Gutiérrez. The Theology of Liberation that he represents is entirely orthodox." With regard to the problem of the necessary diversity of theologies within the Church, he added: "A condemnation of Gustavo Gutiérrez would have, it is my full conviction, very negative consequences for the climate that is the condition in which a theology that is at the service of evangelization may endure. Today there are diverse schools and it has always been thus. . . . It would be deplorable if this legitimate pluralism were to be restricted by administrative means."

It is not possible for me to determine if this letter, dated March 16, 1984, originated from the vague rumors that were then circulating about a possible condemnation of liberation theology or, more specifically, from a series of negative observations made by the Congregation for the Doctrine of the Faith about Gustavo Gutiérrez and his theology—observations to which Gutiérrez had to respond.

Whatever the case, I believe that Rahner's statement deserves special consideration for four reasons.

The first is the undisputed authority of the one making this statement. It is no secret to anyone that Karl Rahner, even apart from his lengthy and profound works, was one of the theologians who had a most decisive influence on the "doctrinal wealth" of Vatican II which Paul VI mentioned in his closing homily. Rahner, therefore, is an ideal judge of what is or is not in accord with the teachings of the Church's magisterium in the modern, post-conciliar period.

The second reason is that to declare Gutiérrez's liberation theology to be "entirely orthodox" is equivalent to declaring as similarly orthodox the line which stems from him and also relies on him. In effect, despite personal differences between the various Latin American theologians, there is a clear, fundamental agreement on the parameters coordinates established by the work of Gustavo Gutiérrez which gave its name to that theological current. Karl Rahner knew this and, after establishing the orthodoxy of Gutiérrez, affirms that "the theology of liberation *which he represents* is entirely orthodox." Therefore, one could speak of heterodoxy to designate only unilateral or extremist falsifications that seek shelter under the same title.

The third reason has greatest interest for the present reflection. To declare that a theology is *orthodox* does not mean that it is *true*. As far as I know, Karl Rahner never called himself a liberation theologian, nor did he accept all of Gutiérrez's theses. He himself speaks of the limitations which the specific context from which it emerges imposes upon liberation theology—as it does upon any theology. The letter quoted above states this explicitly.

In reality, it is very common in theology to give a technical meaning to the adjective "orthodox" which does not strictly coincide with that of "true." This meaning refers less to the truth of a theology than to the right to exist which a particular interpretation of Christian faith enjoys within a healthy theological pluralism. Whoever speaks of "diverse schools" of theology must presuppose the existence of errors within them because it would not be realistic to suppose that their discrepancies arise only from not having realized that what is missing in one is exactly and precisely present in another. The healthiness, richness, and legitimacy of pluralism (as Rahner says in his letter) implies that the normal way of correcting those errors, is to discuss them. Condemnation is an extraordinary measure which is justified in those also extraordinary cases in which the danger of a general error (and the consequent destruction of the core of faith) necessitates the curtailment of dialogue. *Complete orthodoxy*, as Rahner means it with respect to liberation theology, refers to the fact that *such a danger does not exist*. Karl Rahner, who defended the function of the Vatican magisterium against certain contemporary attacks, cannot be suspected of meaning otherwise and even less of wanting to relativize the function of that same magisterium.

However, this leads us to the fourth reason. If Rahner sees no such danger it is because he does not see that liberation theology is practically negating the Christian faith. If someone, differing from Rahner, understands that it is negating faith, he or she must adduce arguments that go beyond the "sensus communis" in Catholic theology (and belonging to the magisterium does not exempt one from this). In other words, they must develop their own theology to counter the one that commonly seems to be orthodox. I am not saying that this is a moral duty; I am referring to a logical necessity. During the Reformation, the Roman Catholic Church had to develop a theology to oppose, in the name of faith, Lutheran theology, because the latter was saying things which sounded at variance with the current theology of the day. In its study and search, the magisterium rejected some proposed theologies and finally presented another. But in doing so it had to discover its own strategy. It had to support itself by theological arguments and not by the mere reaffirmation of its doctrinal authority. The result was what we still call today "Tridentine theology."

It is precisely the appearance of *new* theological elements that gives rise to this problem. Even before the document being studied here, attention was drawn to the observations which the Congregation had made with regard to the theology of Gustavo Gutiérrez. I am not using the word "new" in a pejorative sense. I am referring to the simple fact that liberation theology has become fairly accustomed to certain negative arguments which it has had to face even in friendly discussions or dialogues. Therefore, one has the impression that already in those observations made concerning Gutiérrez, the focal concerns of the Congregation had been shifted or displaced.

I have the impression (and may Gutavo Gutiérrez forgive me if I am mistaken) that the responses that Gutiérrez provided did not satisfy the Congregation's observations on his work. And although that may not be the case, I must confess that I understood the reason and strength of those observations only in light of the *Instruction* being studied here. My continuing impression is that Gutiérrez, in his responses, understands the observations as having arisen from that theological *sensus communis* to which every theologian is accustomed in what he or she thinks and writes. It is from there that, with good reason, Gutiérrez gathered the most reliable proofs so that, on the objectionable points, his work would fit into the commonly recognized orthodoxy.

But it was in fact from *new* theological bases that the observations were made. In my understanding, the *Instruction on Certain Aspects of the "Theology of Liberation"* sheds sufficient light to recognize, this time, what the Congregation for the Doctrine of the Faith uses as its criterion to settle the relationship between orthodoxy and pluralism. And it *exposes* its arguments, in the double meaning of expose. It exposes them in the sense that it publicly expresses them (as opposed to what happened with the privately communicated observations concerning Gutiérrez), and it also exposes them in the sense of subjecting them to theological critique. It is an attempt, objectively honest, to make explicit the particular theology to which the ordinary magisterium of the Church, through the Congregation for the Doctrine of the Faith, seeks to set narrower limits for its demands and denunciations than what previously had been recognized as the boundaries of orthodoxy. In what follows, I will try honorably to respect, as I have already said and repeated, the competency of the ordinary magisterium to attempt this. But, with the same sincerity, I hope to be able to review each one of those arguments and the overarching theology that grounds them.

2

Liberation and Secularism

How are we to read the Vatican *Instruction* on liberation theology? A quick glance demonstrates that it is divided into two almost-equal parts. The first part contains six chapters and resembles a lengthy introduction—beyond the brief foreword of two or three pages that appears at the beginning of the document.

At the end of this first part, it says: "In this present document, we will. . . ." It continues with the rest of the chapters, VII through XI, where, one would suppose, it will deal with the two arguments with which it criticizes liberation theology or, at least, certain of its products: "uncritically borrowing from Marxist ideology and [having] recourse to theses of a biblical hermeneutic marked by rationalism" (VI,10).

But whoever accepts this division of the document (between an informative introduction and a body of argumentation) reads it wrongly. Why? Basically because when the words "we will" appear, despite the future tense, liberation theology has already been condemned and, what is more, the *theological reasons* have already been expounded for such a condemnation.[1]

A General Picture

The entire structure of the document logically depends on its purpose. According to the Introduction, this purpose is "to draw the attention of pastors, theologians, and all the faithful to the deviations, and risks of deviation, damaging to the faith and to Christian living, that are brought about by certain forms of liberation theology. . . ." Therefore, it deals with—and the Introduction itself states this fearlessly—an end "limited" to the *negative* that exists in that theology or at least in its more or less characteristic forms. Otherwise, it would make no sense to place those forms under the title of liberation theology.

Before proceeding, a brief reflection upon this negative limitation —which the document itself offers as a key to its reading—is needed.

First, I believe, we must make a serious effort not to confuse this key, as it is expressed, with ill will. As painful as it may be for the pastors, theologians, and the faithful who adhere more or less consciously and lucidly to liberation theology, one must recognize that the document means to respond for the good of the Church. It points out, then, the negative and only the negative—above all in a case that it considers an emergency, at least in principle—with the view of warning against a current of opinion. Its purpose is, as the document proclaims, to warn against the "deviations and risks" that it considers very serious. If one agrees on the existence of such deviations, then the warning, with all its one-sidedness, is logical. It would not make much sense for a non-academic work to surround this red "danger!" sign with nuances, praises, or even the recognition of the possible merits of liberation theology in its more acceptable forms.

Second, it is surprising to see the presence of various positive elements—although vaguely called principles—which are attributed to liberation theology in the odd-numbered chapters of the first part of the document. It is even more surprising since the Introduction promises a later document where (as opposed to the present *Instruction*) "the vast theme of Christian freedom and liberation . . . in a positive fashion" will be treated.

In my view, the document gives two reasons why it expressly mentions those positive elements when its purpose is to warn against deviations and risks. The first reason stems from the perception of the opposite danger: "a disavowal of all those who want to respond generously and with an authentic evangelical spirit to the 'preferential option for the poor.'" The second reason is implicit in the fact that the diverse forms of liberation theology equally affect "pastors, theologians, and the faithful." At first glance, one could think that the *Instruction* concerns theologians exclusively. However, the Congregation for the Doctrine of the Faith knows very well that in practice liberation theology, even more so than other theologies, reaches all strata of the Christian people in many ways. And for this document to capture the negative element that constitutes the danger, it is necessary to explain in some way what this theology is and how it stems from Christian faith. This is so that later it can show how it has deviated. This negative part will occupy the even-numbered chapters of the document's first part.

It seems to me, third, hermeneutically unsound and unfaithful to take the positive elements (in the odd-numbered chapters) out of their obvious and explicitly "negative" context and thus *save* the theology of liberation. The same holds true to pretend that the negative elements, and not the positive ones, are what characterize that theology as it exists among us. Furthermore, I think that to read the *Instruction* correctly, and therefore as a specific hermeneutic principle (even for the odd-numbered chapters), one must always suppose that the *apparently* positive or neutral observations are destined, according to the expressed intention of the document, to show how an evangelical element has nevertheless resulted in "reducing" that same Gospel to an "earthly" message (VI,4-5).

To give a single example, the document speaks about the interpretation that must be made of the great prophets of Israel, and ends this subject with these words: "Justice as regards God and justice as regards mankind are inseparable. God is the defender and the liberator of the poor" (IV,6). Any liberation theologian would subscribe to such words and would even ask what interest the document could have in making its own one of the most typical and central emphases of that theology. If we apply the principle we are talking about, we will understand (correctly) that these words actually accuse the theology of liberation of separating the justice owed to humanity from that which concerns God and of "reducing" the latter to the former. That is why it says it is God—and not humanity—who defends and liberates the poor.

This is how we will discover what "deviation" can be perceived in liberation theology; at the same time we will be able to discern the theology that generates this negative perception or evaluation. And, vice versa, if we take pains to minimize the criticism of liberation theology by taking into account any text that appears favorable to it, the entire criticism in the *Instruction* will seem to be an exaggeration, and we will continue to ignore what it is in reality: a *different* theological interpretation of the Christian message is supported by magisterial authority. Deriving from this very serious "difference," the document attacks "developments of that current of thought which, under the name 'theology of liberation,' proposes a *novel* interpretation of both the content of faith and of Christian existence which seriously departs from the faith of the Church and, in fact, actually constitutes a practical negation" (VI,9).

Fourth, through a process that the *Instruction* wants to make clear and thus denounce, it is asserted that liberation theology—departing from the intrinsic elements of Christian faith (see the odd-numbered chapters)—gradually deviated from the whole faith, reducing it and virtually negating it. That is why the *Instruction* states that this process is not accidental. *All* theology that takes this path is seen as pulled in two directions: one toward the voice of Puebla which asks one to opt preferentially for the poor, and the other toward the temptation to make that option simpler and more effective by reducing this option to one for the world and for history. "The different theologies of liberation are situated between the *preferential option for the poor,* forcefully reaffirmed without ambiguity after Medellín at the Conference of Puebla on the one hand, and the temptation tó reduce the Gospel to an earthly gospel on the other" (VI,5).

This speçtrum—within which all liberation theologies should fall —with its two extremes and obvious shades in between, is the element that clearly and logically structures the first six (theological) chapters of the document. Liberation is an authentic and evangelical "aspiration" and constitutes one of the principal signs of the times (I); *but* it has "expressions" where one must exercise discernment lest that aspiration be monopolized by ideologies and end up serving almost any cause (II). Liberation and even the theology of liberation —insofar as it is "a special concern for the poor and the victims of oppression which in turn begets a commitment to justice," "centered on the biblical theme of liberation and freedom"—is perfectly valid and "elicits a strong and fraternal echo" (III); *but* this "first point of reference" has "biblical themes" that must be correctly illuminated by exegesis and theology; otherwise it will "set out on a road which leads to the denial of the meaning of the person and his or her transcendence" (IV). "In order to answer the challenge levelled at our times by oppression and hunger, the Church's Magisterium has frequently expressed . . . the present urgency of the doctrine and imperatives contained in Revelation" and "the relationship between freedom from oppression and full freedom, or the salvation of humanity" (V); *but* "the zeal and the compassion which should dwell in the hearts of all pastors nevertheless runs the risk of being led astray and diverted to works which are just as damaging to the human person and his or her dignity as is the poverty which is being fought" and of reducing the Gospel "to a purely earthly gospel" (VI).

It is in this way that the first six chapters develop the real and basic theological argument against liberation theology through their repeated seesaw between the two extremes of the spectrum—the Christian message and its reduction to humanism. If this is so (as I believe it is), the fate of liberation theology has already been determined when the document announces what it *will* discuss. Chapters seven through the final chapter are, in reality, consequences and examples of what has already been treated in the first part: the use of Marxist analysis and of rationalistic exegesis of the Bible.

Because something so important has been totally blown out of proportion by the sensationalism of the press and even passed over by the few theological studies I have seen, I hope the reader will allow me to make a brief analysis of the first paragraphs that begin the second part of the document.

Precisely because Christian faith has been reduced, according to the document, to an earthly humanism, it is incapable of exercising its power of discernment and of guarding Christians against the ideologies that falsely promise results in the search for liberation within history. The most notorious and most seductive of these ideologies is Marxism—perhaps because it foreshadows a possible victory of elements similar to Christian ideals (see IX,10). What is decisive about this point is that what the document considers to be a fall into or "refuge" in ideology is explained as an *effect*, and not as the cause, of a desperate search for earthly results. So the arrival at such a point has, according to the document, a theological *cause*.

The "urgency of the problems" and "the feeling of anguish" (VI,3) generate "impatience and a desire for results"; and this finally leads Christians to "turn to . . . Marxist analysis" (VII,1). "Their reasoning is this: an intolerable and explosive situation requires *effective action* which cannot be put off. Effective action presupposes a *scientific analysis* of the structural causes of poverty. Marxism now provides us with the means to make such an analysis, they say. Then one simply has to apply the analysis to the third-world situation, especially in Latin America" (VII,2).

One can see then that a faith which exercises "discernment" as to how the aspiration for justice and the liberation from evil should be expressed will not be the captive of ideologies. The recourse to Marxism as the instrument of analysis or, as the document states, "taking refuge in it," is nothing more than an example—favored by historical circumstances—of how a faith weakened by and reduced to an earthly content is incapable of resisting ideological temptations.

Theologically speaking, it is of little importance that Marxist analysis itself or the relationship that liberation theology has with it either agrees with reality or deforms it, because the theological judgment does not depend on this fact. *Any* ideological captivation of faith implies that faith has deviated. Moreover, instead of hearing the voice of God in the search for liberation, humanity is merely listening to earthly urgencies to which it attributes the values proper only to the divine word.

Now we must place the emplasis where the document places it: in the reduction and deviation of faith to the earthly. What arguments form the basis of this negative judgment? From what theological perspective is liberation theology viewed so that it is (almost) fatally inclined toward an earthly reductionism? These are the questions that must be answered.

An Inventory Reading

Theological schema. An inventory reading demands that one seek out the signs that point to a system or theological schema from which the theology of liberation may be declared the practical negation of Christian faith.

As stated in the previous chapter, liberation theology has been developing for a quarter of a century, although without that name; and it has been almost fifteen years since it received the name by which it is now known the world over. Under this title its questions, its ideas, and its methodology have been explained. Since then, the principal liberation theologians and, more generally, the pastoral activity and life of the Church in Latin America have been linked to a great extent to this way of doing theology. As with any theological current, some of its theses have been debated. In none of these debates, however, has it seriously been charged that it (or they, since there are sub-tendencies) is heterodox, is a serious deviation from the Christian message. Furthermore, it would be an inadmissable procedure to use the term "liberation theology" or, what is more, "theologies," to point out, in spite of so much serious work, superficialities or deformities present in any school of theological thought. This is why I said that the obvious and total relationship established by the document between liberation theology and heterodoxy demands, logically, the presence of a particular theology in the *Instruction* that allows us to go further in our search.

The inventory reading that we are proposing will therefore consist in reexamining the first (theological) part of the document, looking for signs of that particular theology. Those signs are certainly present but are not always explicit—and even are they grouped together and systematized. To present these signs in systematic fashion will be our second task—in which the reader will have to forgive unavoidable repetitions.

Right at the beginning of the Introduction, we find a significant antinomy. It states that "liberation is first and foremost liberation from the radical slavery of sin." In view of this, the "urgency of the problems" provokes the temptation "to emphasize, unilaterally, the liberation from servitude of an earthly and temporal kind."

Three elements here are worthy of consideration. The first is that opposition (for the moment, at least) is established between two different "emphases"—between an emphasis on the "radical" and, through it, on what will be the result, and an emphasis on the "secondary" which, by setting aside the root (*radix*), will achieve only "one-sided" or partial aspects of liberation. Radical aspects cannot be called partial because, going to the root of the problem, they lead to complete liberation. On the other hand, everything that does not touch the root of the matter, emphasizing only this or that, is partial or one-sided.

The second element, which we have already mentioned, is that the radical is not as visible as are the consequences, where the "urgency of the problems" is perceived. The temptation that is mentioned stems from the difficulty of abandoning the realm of the tangible, which also attracts and urges, to delve into and arrive at a less evident realm where the urgencies give way to the valid in a permanent or definitive way.

However, much more important than these two elements is the third, which lends its most explicit theological meaning to the opposition between the slavery "of sin" and "earthly and temporal" servitudes. The realm of the invisible, because it belongs to the root of reality, to the realm of causes, is opposed to the realm of the visible where consequences flourish. Thus, the cause is "sin"; the consequences are "earthly and temporal" servitudes.

Let us look at an example in order to see this opposition more clearly. Faced with the difficulties and problems plaguing the people of Nicaragua, if we affirm that we must be aware of the incidence of sin for their solution, most people will not understand what we mean. "Sin" belongs to a sphere of language (and of reality) different from the one in which the question was formulated. And if we insist on knowing what type of question would be answered by pointing out that sin causes the problems, the unanimous response would be that the question belongs to the "religious" sphere. The original problem, order. Hence the difficulty in understanding the language of sin without translation.

We do not pretend that this answer is exact. But the entire matter emphasizes an undeniable linguistic fact: there exists one language for speaking of *religious* realities (sin, grace, etc.) and another for secular, earthly, or temporal realities.

Whoever admits this obvious fact, and who begins to ask about the more visible problems (receiving as a response that the root of the problems lies in the slavery to sin) can and should give to that response one of two meanings: (a) the given solution supposes that fighting sin, as a religious reality is a totally adequate answer (and everything else will be obtained as a consequence); or (b) the word "sin" should, without abandoning its religious context, be translated in such a way that it points to realities—individual as well as social—that are concretely expressed outside of the religious sphere.

The reader versed in the theological works of Latin America knows that liberation theology (agreeing with the *Introduction* of the document which states that radical slavery is what ties humanity to sin) makes use of the second of the meanings given above.

At this point in our analysis we are not commenting about the theology of the document; we thus leave that issue open. But, before proceeding, let the reader be advised that the same basic opposition will be found at the crucial point where the document is divided into its two parts. And it is found there because, as in the *Introduction*, the central argument hinges on it.

The *Introduction* speaks of the "feeling of anguish at the urgency of the problems," as though these latter were opposed to the "essential."[2] It refers to the "urgency of sharing bread," as a temptation, to "evangelization" (VI,3) "rooted in the Word of God, correctly interpreted" (VI,7) and not reduced "to a purely earthly gospel" (VI,4-5). It is precisely in the face of earthly structures that there appear "the impatience and desire for results" (VIII,1) which will lead the theologies of liberation to deviate ideologically and to "take refuge," uncritically, in analytical methods of historical reality such as Marxism (see VII, 2ff).

We will return later in our analysis—and with more criteria for judgment—to this very place in the document; but we must now reexamine the beginning sections. There we find a chapter (odd-numbered) aimed at showing that the "aspiration" for liberation constitutes one of the "principal signs of the times which the Church has to examine and interpret in the light of the Gospel" (I,1). In terms of the different forms in which that aspiration is manifested, the document presents a list which coincides point by point with one that might be found in any of the theologies of liberation. It speaks of "a variety of different oppressions: cultural, political, racial, social and economic, often in conjunction with one another" (I,2); that is, they add to or multiply one another because of their interrelationship.

Moreover, implying the positive role of certain conflicts with regard to these diverse oppressions that society often tries to hide, the document admits that the Gospel (among other factors) has "contributed to an awakening of the consciousness of the oppressed" and has thus emphasized a conflict that in many respects and places was ignored (I,4).

It then graphically details the principal elements of those oppressions: the failure to use all of the means available today to alleviate the population explosion (I,5); the scandal of the inequality between rich and poor, and between social classes in a single society as well as on an international level (I,6); the lack of equity in transnational commerce that results in the exploitation of third-world countries (I,7); colonialism and its effects (I,8); the arms race which, while endangering world peace, leads to exorbitant expenditures of wealth that could have been used to "respond to the needs of those people who want for the basic essentials of life" (I,9).

Given this list, it cannot be said (and I think it is evident) that the interest so manifested by liberation theology in these "temporal" oppressions is not shared in its sociopolitical entirety by the document. It is true that, dealing with an odd-numbered chapter, one must wait for the following chapter to determine what the critical difference is between the way of focusing upon these "signs of the times" utilized by liberation theology and the way favored by the document.

However, a close reading manifests a dissonant note in the use of the very term "signs of the times," at least in terms of how the theology of liberation normally uses it. The document uses an exegetical interpretation of that phrase which is not the most common, and which makes possible a later criticism. According to the text, this irresistible aspiration of the people for liberation constitutes one of the principal signs of the times "which the Church has to *examine and interpret in the light of the Gospel.*"

For the moment, it is enough to ask—and this is not an eccentric subtlety—if the two verbs "examine" and "interpret" mean the same thing or if both (or only the latter) refer to the circumstantial complement "in the light of the Gospel."[3] The following chapter of the document, dealing successively with "discernment" (II,2-3) and "interpretation" (II,4) of the signs of the times, does not answer the question. It is certain that in the document only the second task, that of interpretation, applies to "in the light of the Gospel." However, the discernment necessary for knowing which "expressions" are authentic aspirations and which ones are "captive of ideologies" needs to be "clarified and guided," without a doubt, by something superior to what constitutes the "signs of the times" alone. The option between one or the other makes one suppose that discernment should also be done in the light of the Gospel. In any event, I believe that the special use that the document makes of the expression "the signs of the times" is one of the theological indicators that the present critical reading must not fail to point out.

In effect, in the three synoptic Gospels, the term—or rather the need for a "sign" or signal to discern if Jesus possessed and brought a divine message or revelation—is linked to a negative on the part of Jesus. He is not willing to give to his contemporaries, and in particular to the *experts on the interpretation of God's law or revelation*— those who demand such signs—a *sign from heaven* (Mk 8:11-13).

To the implicit objection (made explicit at the beginning of the polemic) that they cannot exercise a (theological) discernment between a divine presence and a diabolical one, Jesus would have responded, according to Q, that *they already possessed* a sufficient criterion: the signs of the times, according to Matthew (16:3) or the present time, according to Luke (12:56).

The Gospel does not tell us directly what manner of discernment this is, but it does indicate one of its primary characteristics—the signs of the times are not subject to an ulterior or superior criterion or discernment, as Jesus' adversaries held. This is understood very clearly, first, through two comparisons of Q:[4] the knowledge that one has of future events through present climatic conditions. Thus the evangelists establish the comparison between two different weather predictions and conclude, according to Matthew: "If you know how to interpret [without additional criteria] the look of the sky, can you not read [do you need an additional criterion to interpret] the signs of the times?" (16:3). Luke adds: "Why do you not judge *for your-selves* [that is, without seeking a higher criterion] what is just?" (12:57).

Second, to show that his generation already has sufficient signs without needing to consult the Bible (or, obviously, the Gospel), Jesus poses, as examples of discernment favorably judged by God, what *pagans* did. Therefore, "at the preaching of Jonah" the inhabitants of Nineveh, like the queen of the South before "the wisdom of Solomon," discerned better than those who possessed the written word of God. In Jesus' argument, then, the signs of the times and the response to them constitute a presupposition for the correct reading of the Word, and not vice versa.[5]

Because of all this, as significant for the Gospel period as for our day, it is important to point out the strange use the document makes of the evangelical expression "the signs of the times," a use which is directly contrary to Jesus' own use: that is, as something that is not clear in itself and that must pass through the crucible of another, superior discernment—the light of the Gospel. The radicalness of Jesus' approach lies precisely in demanding a historical (or secular) sensitivity toward one's neighbor's need. It is only that openness or sensitivity from the heart (the seat of discernment, in biblical language) that can serve as the hermeneutical presupposition for a correct reading of the Word of God (see Mk 2:27; 3:5) and, therefore, for encountering and using the light of the Gospel. Anything else could lead to the Gospel's own negation, like the Old Testament read by the Pharisees and used as the criterion of discernment in Jesus' case. The function of the signs of the times is precisely that of helping one break the circle of the dead letter—even in the case of the Gospel.

But we must continue with our inventory reading. Chapter II of the *Instruction* begins by exercising this necessary discernment. In effect, while the aspiration for liberation is perfectly compatible with the Gospel, according to the document, it is not equally the case with all "the theoretical and the practical manifestations of this aspiration" (II,2).

We should, then, ask ourselves what is or may be introduced between the generic (correct) aspiration and its (ambiguous) expressions. The answer that we find in this part of the document is incomplete but significant: "the aspiration for justice often finds itself the captive of ideologies which hide or pervert its meaning" (II,3).

The word "often" would not make much sense if the text were not seeking to point out a more or less mechanical link between the aspiration for justice on the one hand and its hiding or perversion on the other. However, one could propose that the aspiration for justice has nothing that might make it more susceptible than any other correct aspiration to being hidden or perverted when one seeks to put it into practice. The reason for making such a more or less mechanical link might be the simple fact that liberation theology is characterized as based on that aspiration. In this way, instead of using "liberation theology," the document would use synonyms ("aspiration for justice") that characterize it. There are two reasons, however, that militate against this hypothesis.

The first reason is explicit. After speaking in the previous chapter of the aspiration for liberation as one of the principal signs of the times, and without touching upon the theme of the theology that would make this aspiration its own, the second chapter begins by specifically mentioning the theme of justice and relating it to certain dangers: "The yearning for justice and for the effective recognition of the dignity of every human being needs, like every deep aspiration, to be clarified and guided" (II,1).

It is true the incisive "like every deep aspiration" tends to take away from *this* specific aspiration a special connection to dangers and deformities from which other deep aspirations would be seen as safe. For it is clear that, according to the document, all the signs of the times, and not only those that point to liberation theology, must fall under the discernment of the Gospel.

Even so, I believe that this attempt to equate all deep aspirations does not work. It only says that they are *often* linked to hiding and perversion. It does not seem probable that the document would be open to saying the same thing of *any* deep aspiration, such as the one which leads people to avoid sin and maintain friendly relationships with God. Furthermore, in the paragraph between the two cited, something very important is said that exposes where the *Instruction's* real concern lies: "there are many political and social movements which present themselves as authentic spokesmen for the aspirations of the poor" (II,2). In other words, such movements are apparently guided by the same aspiration for justice. I believe it is obvious that one must, seek there, in those political and social movements, the mechanism by which the aspiration for justice (and no other, no matter how deep it may be) often is captivated by ideologies that hide or pervert its meaning.

But there is also a second reason, logically linked to the first, by which one must attribute a specific danger of ideological captivation to the aspiration for justice. The *Introduction* makes the fundamental distinction between *radical* liberation—from sin—and liberation "from the servitudes of a temporal kind." I have already pointed out that this distinction would be equivalent to the one that exists between two planes of language, the religious and the secular. Therefore, even a quick reading of the document will show that in its view the radical struggle against sin—and this would apply equally to religious terms such as "conversion of heart," "redemption," "the search for individual perfection," "practicing virtue," etc.—is never in danger of being captivated by ideologies.

On the other hand, in many places in the document this ideological captivation (or the risk of falling into it) is associated with the "urgency" of entering into liberating struggles in the temporal or profane order. Note one of the clearer passages, with special reference to the situation in Latin America: "In certain parts of Latin America, the seizure of the vast majority of the wealth by an oligarchy of owners bereft of social consciousness, the practical absence or the shortcomings of a rule of law, military dictators making a mockery of elementary human rights, the corruption of certain powerful officials, the savage practices of some foreign capital interests constitute factors which nourish a passion for revolt among those who thus consider themselves the powerless victims of a new colonialism in the technological, financial, monetary or economic order" (VII,12). The paragraph is not only terribly correct; it is also tremendously eloquent and, taken out of context and placed in a political tract, would elicit warm applause and enthusiastic cheers. But the document goes on: "The recognition of injustice is accompanied by a *pathos* which borrows its language from Marxism."

As is evident, ideological captivation also appears here. And one perceives that the frequency of that negative result is related to the "pathetic" strength of the aspiration for justice, added to the consciousness that justice does not exist. Why would *radical* liberation, or any other of the religious elements mentioned above, be free of that *pathos?* By going directly to the root—to that which is not apparent but hidden and profound—the religious has a fundamental advantage over the profane: its immunity to ideological captivation which uses human passions for its ends.

At the present stage in our reading, there is still a hypothesis that will have to be verified or falsified in what follows, and already has its first application in another aspect of the text. In effect, for the first time, we meet the noun "ideology" (the adjective "ideological" appeared twice before in the Introduction). It is true that we have managed the preceding without knowing exactly what the document means by this word. We have only perceived that it has a negative significance and that it appears in conjunction with "political and social movements" of which Marxism has been explicitly mentioned. It would be possible to add a somewhat vague but important element with regard to faith, that is, to elements that the Christian takes from the Gospel. Ideology appears as something that silently or unconsciously infiltrates it, deforming it, and leading it to results that no longer correspond to its initial intention.

Keeping in mind, then, that "ideology" seems to be an important word for the criticism of liberation theology and also that its usage by the document does not seem to coincide with the one commonly used in technical language (philosophy, sociology of knowledge, e.g.), we must stop here and try to ascertain how we should perceive the word in order to understand the document more properly.

It seems evident that one must exclude the possibility that it uses the word "ideology" (or the corresponding adjective) in the more usual negative sense that it has in some types of sociology. In what comes directly from Marx and, more generally, in any discussion of socioeconomic interests, the word has a very clear meaning: ideology is a falsification of reality, destined (more or less unconsciously in the majority of cases) to hide and, as such, validate unjust, contradictory, and inhuman aspects of society. If I hold, for example, that the Latin American worker is lazy—without taking into account the quantity and quality of his food or the hopes of substantially improving his life which his income may offer—I will be told that I am using an *ideological* argument. More subtly, the mere fact of pretending to be neutral in, or indifferent to, an important conflict is considered ideological because (even unconsciously) to relativize a real conflict is to side with those who are in a superior position in that conflict.

There are two ways of thinking which, by definition, do not fall within this understanding of the ideological. They are, on the one hand, those thoughts or systems of ideas that struggle for the interests of the people whom society oppresses or marginalizes. If the systems are used effectively, their articulation will overcome the (false) arguments used to prop up the *status quo*.

Of course, this does not mean that, not being ideological, such thinking is *correct;* it only means that it has avoided the trap of the lie. (One may defend a good cause with false arguments.) Nor does this mean that such thinking is *impartial;* it is partial and biased, but unlike "ideological" arguments, it is conscious of its own partiality. Going against the current, it cannot hide its partiality from itself or from others. And this in itself is good though it may never be definitive: if that partiality wins, is imposed, and is generalized, it will surely produce its own ideological elements.

Note, finally, that (in strict logic and whether or not Marx would agree) religious thought can play an ideological as well as an anti-ideological role. For example, a religious thought will be ideological if it makes the oppressed believe that God wishes their oppression. And the "leaven of the Gospel" will be anti-ideological if it, in the words of the document, "has contributed to an awakening of the consciousness of the oppressed" (I,4).

There is a second type of thinking or system of thought, on a more abstract (and epistemological) level, that escapes this first use of the term "ideology." It is the system that develops mental tools to detect and combat everything that is "ideological" in a culture. Returning to the previous example of the supposed laziness of the Latin American worker, a system of thought that accustoms us not to make generic moral judgments without first taking into account the basic conditions in which the people live and work—whether or not such judgments are correct—is anti-ideological. A critical method that leads us to suspect the "happy ending" of movies (which anesthetize our culture) is anti-ideological. And finally (so that there may be no doubt about this important point) Marx's historical materialism, whether or not we agree with it, is by its very intention and method an anti-ideological system of thought.

This is, then, one of the understandings of the word. It has a *strict* and *negative* use. Its use is strict because it is not applied indiscriminately to any thought or system of thought. It is negative because it is applied only to a deformation of reality, provoked unconsciously by interests created within society. In this understanding, ideology means *false social consciousness*.

There is, however, a second and wider understanding of the word "ideology," more proper to ordinary language. Ideology is often understood as any system of thought situated on a more elevated and general level than that of science. It would represent almost a philosophical view of reality (especially of human reality) if the term "philosophy" were not almost always reserved for purely theoretical systems. The word "ideology," on the contrary, is almost always on the middle ground between theory and practice.

We are discussing the meaning of the term "ideology" because we are faced with it in this second chapter of the document. The reader may remember that in the previous paragraph, already cited, there appeared something that must be almost a synonym for what the document understands by ideology: "political and social movements." These have, in effect, a philosophy about human life and the best way of living it in society; but at the same time, they are characterized as "movements" for having established methods of analysis and action to put into practice those conceptions of the world and of the individual that characterize them. Thus one speaks of capitalist, socialist, Christian Democratic, and ecologist ideology, of the "death of ideologies" which are outdated in view of other urgencies, and so on.

It should be clear that this new understanding of the word "ideology" is very distinct from the *precise* and *negative* one that was treated earlier. This second definition is *general* and *neutral*. It is general because every type of system of thought and action falls within it, whether ideological or anti-ideological. It is neutral because the word does not attempt to classify systems as good or bad, true or false. It simply alludes to the fact that people are grouped and divided by distinct systems of thought and action.

Now then, I believe the second definition is not that which the document attempts to give to the word "ideology." I sense the document is dealing with a relatively recent use of the term, one proper to theology and (I would even dare say) proper to a particular theology. This is not the place to investigate the origin of that special use of the word, but only to clarify the reality to which it refers.

In the document the word appears always, or almost always, in relation to religious *faith*. It seems to say that faith becomes ideological when it has lost its character as faith to become a merely human thought. In other words, we are once again up against the problem of two languages, the religious and the secular. What for a secular language has a merely neutral meaning acquires in religious language a pejorative connotation. What is merely human for the former is *too* human for the latter. The use of the term thus becomes a bit esoteric, a privatized language, but not an unintelligible one. It means something very particular and so has synthesized the other two understandings of the word. "Ideology" thus acquires a *general* and *negative* meaning.

It is *general* because it touches upon, like the second understanding, what is most common: all of those systems of thought and action that are distinct from religious faith and stem from the human aspirations to concretely transform the earth and society. It is *negative* because the principal characteristic of ideology, in its first pejorative understanding—being a deformation of reality because of the inherent *partiality* of every human project and interest—has been applied to *every* "all-embracing" (VII,13) system of thought. Every human system is epistemologically partisan (see VII,5-6; VIII,4-5), although this partiality is most patent in Marxism (with its explicit

conception of class struggle as the central element influencing the
very analysis of reality).

It is therefore clear that when reality is analyzed with partiality—
something that the social sciences (whether or not they are Marxist)
cannot escape because that limitation flows from their very nature
(VII,13)—it ends by imposing violently on a part of human social
reality what it attempts to justify in the name of a "global" demand.
That is the fundamental relationship between the captivation of faith
by ideologies and the "recourse to violent means to bring about the
radical changes which will put an end to the oppression and misery of
people" (II,2), "ways of action which imply the systematic recourse
to violence, contrary to any ethic which is respectful of persons"
(II,3).

To finish with the semantic trail of "ideology" and to unite it with
the previous one of the "signs of the times," it is important to make
an observation about the last paragraph of Chapter II. There is, in
my view, a clear contrast regarding the use and meaning of the noun
"ideology" and the adjective "ideological." On the one hand, the
abundant (at times surprising and always negative) use that the
document makes of these terms seems to come from a radical pessi-
mism about the epistemological possibilities of the human being. It
implies that people, attracted by the earthly and always partisan, are
not capable of anything other than a knowledge of a reality that is
urgent, unilateral, deviate, and (in practice) violent. On the other
hand, to this pessimistic view of reality is opposed a supremely idealistic "should be": "The first condition for any analysis is a total
openness to the reality to be described" (VII,13). In the eyes of the
social sciences, this assertion would seem to be the fruit of an un-
measured optimism bordering on epistemological naiveté.

However, that would be a mistake in our judgment since it does
not take into account a special knowledge that, apart from the social
sciences, makes possible the apparently impossible—a special
knowledge that the document calls the "light of the Gospel." This
light (if I understand correctly) frees thought from the analyses that
obey partialities and unilateral interests, and that generate
urgencies, impatience, and the desire for results in the temporal and

earthly sphere, whatever the cost. On the contrary, this illumination of faith, leading us to the profound and invisible reality that transcends the human and directly links people to God, allows for what ideologies will never achieve: a correct view, impartial and dispassionate (without *pathos*) that will be manifested not through violent means but in changes "respectful of persons . . . who have to be converted by the grace of Jesus Christ" (II,4; IV,15; see IV,7). Therefore, the "signs of the times" are not the mere human aspirations surveyed by the social sciences but rather those that pass through a "critical discernment" stemming from that superior and religious epistemological criterion that is the "light of the Gospel."

With this we arrive at chapter III. Like the other odd-numbered chapters, it seems to contain nothing negative about liberation theology; to the contrary, it gives two *positive* definitions of it. According to the first, the expression "theology of liberation" refers to "a special concern for the poor and the victims of oppression, which in turn begets a commitment to justice" (III,3). According to the second definition, it "designates a theological reflection centered on the biblical theme of liberation and freedom, and on the urgency of its practical realization" (III,4).

We are advised, however, that these definitions "present diverse theological positions" and that even the interpretation of the biblical theme of liberation "can be understood only in light of the specific message of Revelation, authentically interpreted by the Magisterium of the Church" (III,4). The two following chapters, "Biblical Foundations" and "The Voice of the Magisterium," follow from this, and the final result will be the negative conclusions of Chapter VI.

As will be seen later (see VI,7), chapter III proposes positive definitions of liberation theology with the aim of showing that the magisterium of the Church, far from being insensitive to this theme, has already developed it correctly and sufficiently—the "authentic theology of liberation" (VI,7)—which leaves room only for a negative judgment about other "theologies of liberation."

At first glance, little can be gained from a study of those positive definitions, they being almost nominal and therefore extremely vague. There is in the first one, however, an element that stands out.

The document takes the expression coined by the episcopal magisterium of the Puebla Conference, "the preferential option for the poor" and gives it a slightly different formulation: "a special concern for the poor and the victims of oppression." Is there not a subtle change of meaning between the two expressions?

The problem becomes deeper and more significant if it is noted that Puebla already modified slightly the formula used until then (and even by many until now) of "the option for the poor." Even more, although the last part of the formulation is usually ignored, Puebla adds to the *preferential* option for the poor the phrase "and for the young." And it is interesting that the present document attacks gently but expressly the "theologies of liberation" for citing Puebla without that significant addition (see VI,6).

Thus, we have four different expressions to compare: (a) option for the poor; (b) preferential option for the poor; (c) preferential option for the poor and the young; and finally, (d) special concern for the poor.

For the moment, if we compare the first three expressions with (d), we will find a significant substitution: "concern" has taken the place of "option." There is a marked difference between these two words when there is a conflict such as the one described by the document in Chapter I and which it summarizes in an even more dramatic way in the already-cited paragraph VII,12. To be specially concerned is not the same as to opt.

To opt (or to choose sides) in a conflict means to enter into it and to accept the inherent partisanship of one of the two sides—in this case, that of the poor. Every option limits. And that limitation is even greater, the deeper and more crucial the conflict. But at the same time the strength and efficacy of the option comes precisely from its partiality.

However, as we take the path from (a) to (d), the strong and conflictive meaning of the word "option" clearly vanishes. In this context it is easy to see that the term "preferential" in Puebla implies a compromise between two theological tendencies, one which is subtle because "option" remains and "preferential" seems to be almost a weak synonym placed there like a pleonasm—a

strange and unnecessary repetition. But in reality it is not a pleonasm; it is as if to say we opt for the poor AND the rich (because the
Church belongs to all) but we give preference to the poor. It is clear
that this implies a curious position in the struggle. It also makes it
difficult to understand the meaning that the Beatitudes[6] would have
if they said "Happy are the poor because preferentially theirs is the
Kingdom of God."[7]

In other words, whoever says "preferential" is logically obligated
to give "option" a conceptual content different from the normal one.
Instead of entering into a struggle and taking part on one of the
sides, it merely means a directed concern. What type of concern?

Expression (c) will help us find a new element enabling us to
respond to that question. At the same time it will provide a new step
on the path of compromise between the two different theologies at
the Puebla Conference. "Preferential option for the poor and the
young" completely removes from the mind the image suggested by
the "option" in a conflict. It indicates that the root cause of the
preference is no longer the dehumanization that the victims of
oppression suffer because "the young" (as opposed to the poor) do
not have a visible or direct relationship with oppression. One must
admit, therefore, that the document is exact and, even more, strictly
logical when it points out a general repugnance (among theologians,
pastors, and lay people) within liberation theology to using the
expression which includes the poor AND the young in the same
preferred option or concern.[8]

Obviously, it is a fact that the option—toward both groups—
cannot be conceived as having the goal of removing poverty from the
shoulders of those who are forced by oppression to carry it (for what
of the young?). If the young deserve preferential attention or concern, it must be because of their special problems, so often passed
over in a dialogue made even more difficult by a generation gap
accentuated by rapid cultural and social change. The problem is not
rooted in the fact that the young may be more oppressed than others
by injustice but rather that it is particularly difficult for them to find
a path and meaning for their lives in a world made in another age
and with other parameters. But the poor equally deserve special
attention because it is particularly difficult for them to find meaning

in the midst of the afflictions that are the daily bread of their lives. We are thinking here of "the radical character of the deliverance brought by Christ and *offered to all,* be they politically free or slaves" (IV,13) and, we might add, socially or economically rich or poor.

This lends full meaning to expression (d), showing how a thought, corrected by the document, goes along a path from the unacceptable extreme of (a) toward (d). The special concern for the poor and the young is basically religious, given that "the New Testament does not require some change in the political or social condition as a prerequisite for entrance into this freedom [brought by Christ]" (IV,13).

Now the reader can perceive that the theology of the *Instruction* is very coherent in all of its points, and even in its language, concepts, and expressions, and that it brings into question not only the excesses but the fundamental elements of the theology of liberation.

Biblical exegesis. Chapter IV is the most extensive and explicit in terms of the document's theology. That is because every Christian theology depends on its way of reading the Bible.

Practically every paragraph of this chapter treats a biblical theme of the Old as well as the New Testament. The majority of them are the themes that liberation theology has used, with a brief indication by the document of the authentic interpretation that should be given them (as opposed to that generally given). A few paragraphs refer to other biblical themes, but their treatment here is just the opposite: they are themes which liberation theology passes over, and which the document feels to be important for correcting deviations in that theology.

Our reading here will have a double task. First, it will underline the strange and, at times, clearly distorted exegesis of some biblical texts in the document. Perhaps some of this exegesis could have been considered as merely partial or incomplete in the past. But recently, the clear orientation of the ecclesiastical magisterium—from Pius XII's *Divino Afflante Spiritu* to Vatican II's *Dei Verbum*—has demanded that Catholic exegetes respect the literal meaning, or rather take seriously the intention and the context, as well as the literary genre, of the biblical passages being examined.

However, second, even more than this task, what interests us here is to show that (whether good or bad) the exegesis employed serves a particular theology—the one that dominates the entire document. The reader will understand why I say it is of greater interest to discover and define that theology: it is the only serious and loyal way of respecting the document—whether or not one agrees with its theology. The document deserves the same respect that the magisterium demanded for interpreting biblical texts—to know the intention of its authors.

It is not purely by chance that the first biblical theme treated in the document is one of those closest to the heart of liberation theology—the Exodus. With good reason the document indicates that the meaning of the events narrated in the Old Testament and brought together in that divine act cannot be understood without considering their "purpose" in God's plan (IV,3): guiding Israel on the path that led from liberation from Egyptian slavery to the possession of the Promised Land after prolonged wandering in the desert.

It is surprising, on the other hand, how the document defines that same "purpose." According to it, those events are "ordered to the foundation of the people of God and the Covenant cult celebrated on Mt. Sinai" (IV,3). Of course, the purpose—of the document, not of the Exodus—in making such an observation is *not* surprising. It is very logically and explicitly directed against every attempt to understand that entire series of episodes as "a liberation which is principally or exclusively *political* in nature," an attempt tacitly attributed to liberation theology.

What has happened here (if I am not mistaken) is a too free-and-easy use of numerous, complex, and cautious exegetical works. As is known, at least four major literary sources have been recognized in the narration of the Exodus, although it is not always easy to recognize them in each verse. The three oldest sources—the Yahwist, the Elohist, and the Deuteronomist—together present Yahweh as intervening in favor of the people *who are already his* because of the compassion he feels toward the *inhuman situation* (whether or not it is called political) in which they are living and because of his desire to give them their own land as promised to their ancestors. "The LORD said, 'I have witnessed the affliction of *my people in Egypt* and have heard their cry of complaint against their slave drivers, so I know well what they are suffering. Therefore I have come down *to rescue them from the hands of the Egyptians and lead them* out of that land *into a good and spacious land.* . . . The cry of the Israelites has reached me, and I have truly noted that the Egyptians are *oppressing* them'" (Ex 3:7-9: Yahwist-Elohist tradition; cf. 3:16-17). And in the famous historical Deuteronomic creed: "My father was a wandering Aramean who went down to Egypt with a small household and lived there as an alien. But there he became a nation great, strong and numerous. When the Egyptians maltreated and oppressed us, imposing hard labor upon us, we cried to the LORD, *the God of our fathers,* and he heard our cry and saw our affliction, our toil and our *oppression.* He brought us out of Egypt with his strong hand and outstretched arm, with terrifying power, with signs and wonders; and *bringing us into this country, he gave us this land* flowing with milk and honey" (Dt 26:5-9).

Nowhere in the oldest traditions is there a trace of the document's alleged purpose, "the foundation of the People of God."[9] Only much later was the tradition of Sinai utilized to found the cult that is practiced in the Temple in Jerusalem. And we have to arrive at the last source of the Pentateuch—the Priestly, written during the Exile —to be able to speak of "the Covenant cult celebrated on Mt. Sinai" (cf. Ex 25-31 and 35-40), although we could not speak of this as the *purpose* of the Exodus.[10] There is, furthermore, an ancient prophetic tradition in Israel according to which, because of God's will, there was no sacrificial cult during the entire wandering in the desert (see Amos 5:25; Jer 7:22).

Be that as it may, it seems very daring from an exegetical point of view to *reduce* the meaning of the Exodus (so wide, vague, and rich) to the two elements cited by the document. But in fact, the true meaning and relevance of this reduction must not be measured (as has already been suggested) by its exegetical accuracy, but rather by its theological purpose.

In effect, the document undoubtedly sees (and not without remote foundation in some exaggerated statements of political theology) in the most obvious meaning of the Exodus, the beginning of the tendency to "reduce the Gospel to a purely earthly gospel." That is why it takes the step, perhaps insufficiently serious, toward rectifying what it understands to be a theological deviation which robbed the Exodus of its true religious content. I believe it is doing justice to the document to say that the argument is more theological than exegetical: that the Exodus a priori cannot have a political purpose because it is a revelation of Yahweh. Given the theological premise, we have the exegetical solution.

Paradoxically, its weakness consists in its being a reductionist premise when what must be sought is to avoid just such a reduction. A Bible reduced to the passages that explicitly speak of God or of specifically religious purposes would exclude passages, chapters, and even entire books. The Jerusalem Bible points out that present-day exegesis does not understand the Song of Songs allegorically, as was done in the past—a book that contains no mention of God or of other explicit religious elements. Entire chapters of the history of David reduce all mention of divine will to two verses that attribute to Yahweh the intent (profane) of placing Solomon on the throne that his father had occupied. Why does the magisterium of the Church oblige us to believe that those books and chapters are inspired by God and so contain divine revelation? Without a doubt, because even without being explicitly religious, the treatment of attitudes that seem merely human or secular helps us to understand who God is, what he loves, and whom he prefers.

I believe that here (and this is logical) the document insists upon a particular theology where the religious and the secular are opposed: insists to the extent that a specific revelation of God—whose glory may be, according to Irenaeus's expression, the human person, or, if you prefer, the humanized person—seems to be excluded.

Something similar appears again in the last words of the paragraph. The document, speaking of the Exodus and the way in which it is interpreted, states that "it is significant that the term *freedom* is often replaced in Scripture by the very closely related term, *redemption*" (IV,3). It is assumed that this is significant because those who give the Exodus a "principally or exclusively political" meaning seem to resist using this second synonym; they do not like to present the Exodus in terms of redemption.

Allow me to say frankly and with loyalty (like any child of the Church) that to use this type of argument—though it may be for a good cause—discredits the magisterium that the Congregation for the Doctrine of the Faith represents. And such disparagement does grave evil to the whole Church, which cannot be balanced and fruitful if it does not respect the teaching function of the magisterium.

In effect, the argument here presumes that the purpose of the Exodus cannot be (merely) secular because the Bible often replaces the (secular) word "liberation" with its (religious) synonym "redemption." However, any theologian or exegete of even average competence knows that when the Bible was written (and at the decisive time when it was translated into the Greek) *both words*— "liberation" and "redemption"—had a fully secular meaning. Liberation means more generally the free exit from any situation of captivity or oppression, while redemption means more specifically to pay the necessary price for a slave to be unshackled and set free.

If not for the fact that our societies no longer are familiar with slavery in its formal sense and, therefore, its legal mechanisms, the technical term "redemption" would have fallen into virtual disuse if its metaphorical meaning had not been retained to designate our situation before God after the "redemptive" death of Jesus Christ. An (intentional?) anachronism is committed when it is pretended that the presence of the term "redemption" in the Bible in reference to the Exodus indicates its "religious" purpose and that not wanting to use the term is indicative of the reductionism and secularism of a particular exegesis.[11] It is clear that using "redemption" in its *current* meaning, with regard to the Exodus, would distort the passage.

It is perhaps important to point out that, after the paragraph we have just finished reading (relative to the Exodus), the entire period of the conquest and occupation of the Promised Land and the foundation of the monarchy is passed over, and there is a jump to the time of the Exile and the post-Exilic epoch, which misplaces the prophets chronologically (although it will be mentioned later). That period omitted in the *Instruction* is dominated by the activity of the royal chroniclers, the writer prophets, and the grand historical synthe-

sis that forms the central part of Deuteronomy. The collection of all
of this material is perhaps one of the richest, deepest, and most cre-
ative in the entire Bible. And is, besides, most marked by the attempt
to unite theologically God's plans with the historical events that the
people both suffer and condition.

Beginning with the great crisis of the Exile and the return to the
Promised Land, there seems to be in Israel a lack of interest in history (despite the parenthetical material dealing with the Maccabees
and their struggle). God directs history along inscrutable paths. Thus,
there arises in the Bible the "wisdom" literature—emphasizing
"wisdom," a term that we would translate today as "spiritual life."
Every Israelite is related to God in a most personal way—through
prayer, worship, and the fulfillment of the moral law. When the hope
of change arises, this change is thought of as a transformation that
Yahweh will introduce at the end of history (eschatology or apocalyp-
tic).

Now, with respect to this eschatological perspective, two passages
often cited (although they may not be the passages that best fit
in the context of the most evident biblical eschatology) are the
prophecies about a "new covenant" that Yahweh will make with
Israel, especially Jeremiah 31:31-34 and Ezekiel 36:26ff. The document we are examining dedicates a paragraph to these prophecies
and states that what is promised in them is a reality "marked by the
gift of His Spirit and the conversion of hearts" (IV,4).

But the prophets of the great historical age that precedes the
Exile, and to which we have already referred, do not commonly
insist on this interior dimension. Rather, they customarily project
God's view of the events that have public status. The prophets are
the "guides" of Israel throughout its complex history under the
monarchy. The document recognizes this. When it treats the great
prophets of Israel, it points out that their prophecies "keep affirming
with particular vigor the requirements of justice and solidarity and
the need to pronounce a very severe judgment on the rich who
oppress the poor" (IV,6).

Nevertheless, returning to the Exile and what happened afterwards, the two prophetic texts of Jeremiah and Ezekiel centered,
according to the document, on the "conversion of hearts." And it is

true that these two prophecies speak of hearts and how they will be changed. Jeremiah: "I will place my law within them, and write it upon their hearts. . . . No longer will they have need to teach their friends and kinsmen how to know the Lord. All, from least to greatest, shall know me" (Jer 31:33-34). According to Ezekiel, Yahweh will give the Israelites "a new heart . . ., taking from your bodies your stony hearts and giving you natural hearts" (Ez 36:26).

The intention of the document in citing these two famous prophecies can be made no clearer. It is a correction similar to that already made with regard to the Exodus: liberation theology speaks of economic, social, and political change, while the Bible speaks of the conversion of hearts (individual, "of each person," as Jeremiah says).

Two observations must be made about this exegesis. The first is that, being correct in principle, it should not be separated from its wider context. For example, what does Jeremiah mean when speaking of a heart that "knows the Lord"? One can ask Jeremiah himself, and his response is important and clarifying in his prophecy against the king Jehoiakim: "Woe to him who builds his house on wrong,/ his terraces on injustice;/ Who works his neighbor without pay,/ and gives him no wages. . . ./ Your father [Josiah]/ . . . did what was right and just,/ and it went well with him. Because he dispensed justice to the weak and the poor,/ it went well with him./ *Is this not true knowledge of me?*/ says the Lord" (Jer 22:13-16; emphasis added).

But, once more, what is important is not so much that the document, through its exegesis of the biblical texts which synthesize two dimensions inseparably, reduces them to only one. What is more significant and relevant is that this reductionism is always linked to a very coherent theology whose elements are slowly coming to light. Here, the document is dealing with, as will be seen, the emphasis it places on the single element of "the conversion of hearts." The reason for this emphasis will become even clearer in the following paragraph dealing with the Psalms.

Before going on, I believe it necessary to make a second observation. In seeking to separate these specific prophecies (Jer 31:31 and Ez 36:26) from the paragraph regarding the prophets of Israel (see

IV,6), the document must have had an equally special purpose. I believe it is that the crisis of the Exile awakens a "hope of a new liberation" distinct from that of the Exodus. The oracles of the prophets of Israel, who almost always had as their object defects of the social and religious life of the monarchy, are framed within the Covenant, the old one, that was broken by nonfulfillment of the Law.

To me, it seems easy to conclude that the document separates and focuses upon the prophecies of Jeremiah and Ezekiel because it recognizes in them the announcement of the New Covenant, which is another way of saying the New Testament. The New Covenant will be unbreakable, as opposed to the old one that failed: "It will not be like the covenant I made with their fathers the day I took them by the hand to lead them forth from the land of Egypt; for they broke my covenant" (Jer 31:32). The *conversion of hearts,* carrying within them the written Law and thus making its fulfillment spontaneous, is what will make the New Covenant unbreakable.

Now, it seems important to point out that, as they are formulated, these prophecies of Jeremiah and Ezekiel never were fulfilled. Many other prophecies of the Old Testament were never fulfilled, such as Nathan's prophecy that there would always be a king of the Davidic line seated upon the throne of Jerusalem (2 Sam 7:11-16). The reality of the New Testament is very different from the hope formulated during the Exile, and it is far superior to what was envisioned by Jeremiah and Ezekiel. It therefore becomes theologically very doubtful in what sense their prophecies can truly characterize in a special way the reality of present-day Christians. And if the prophets' vision continues to be a criterion of what must be done, it would merely prove that the prophecy has little bearing on the present and is not something typically Christian that was envisioned only as a hope in ancient Israel.

Let us continue with the document's paragraph relative to the Psalms. Although they do not strictly belong to the wisdom literature, it is not without purpose that they begin, in the oldest arrangement of the biblical books, the part of the "Writings" that follows "the Law and the Prophets" and are characterized by the domination of the wisdom books. Although some of the older psalms still call to mind a past marked by the historical acts of God, the very recompilation of the Psalms took place in an age when, lacking actualization and concrete thought, Israel was becoming a "religion of the heart," of individual worship and piety.

Of course, nothing of what has been said takes anything away from the intrinsic value of the Psalms, theologically speaking. But the very context from which they arose and in which they were compiled explains why the theology of liberation makes less use of them today when we live in a context that is more similar to other times and problems in Israel's history. For that reason, no one today cites Proverbs as much as they do Genesis, or Revelation as often as they do the Gospels. And it is not even necessary to cite a more practical reason: the very books of the New Testament and the practice of twenty centuries of Christianity have created prayers that are more appropriate than the Psalms for specifically Christian message and themes.

Notwithstanding all of this, one cannot omit the fact of liberation theology's lesser interest in the Psalms; and this may be the sign of a particular theological conception. That is why, without a doubt, the document we are studying dedicates a paragraph to the Psalms which is an implicit, yet clear, criticism of that theology. What exegetical elements does the document see in the Psalms? First, it points out that the theme of the majority of the Psalms is that of an anguished person. What is that anguish? It "is not purely and simply equated with the social condition of poverty or with the condition of the one who is undergoing political oppression. It also includes the hostility of one's enemies, injustice, failure, and death" (IV,5).

Certainly there is no doubt that of all the books of the Bible, the Psalms present a greater interiorization or spiritualization. In the Psalms, the human soul—with all its existential problems, its finitude, and its powerlessness—is placed before the greatness and transcendence of God. According to the document, "the Psalms call us back to an essential religious experience: it is from God alone that one can expect salvation and healing. God, and not man, has the power to change the situations of suffering" (IV,5).

If one were to take this paragraph as an absolute truth, liberation theology would collapse. In effect, separating this text from the chapter's other paragraphs (which form its natural context), we would be faced with the most blatant assault on liberation theology's idea of God and of human activity in history. Or, to say it better, one would have to speak of the *non*-activity of people in history because all concrete change concerning human suffering is taken from the human field of action and attributed *only* to God.

I believe there are two reasons for not making this separation, one implicit and one explicit. First, it is important that this paragraph should appear within a context that recognizes different "biblical foundations." The Bible is not reduced to the Psalms. Neither can the relationship between the person and God that is the theme of the majority of the Psalms be taken as the only valid one. One of the hermeneutical principles imposed by the magisterium upon Catholic exegesis is respect for the different literary genres of biblical writings. And one of the most particular and obvious literary genres is that of the Psalms. It is a book of *pleas* or prayers. Therefore, the document cannot ignore that, with the Psalms, it faces a special relationship between God and the individual. It is as special as the situation of suffering that leads the individual to interrupt other activities and seek from God a solution to his or her problems. If one did not observe this precaution with the Psalms, one might likewise conclude from the book of Proverbs that the only basic relationship between God and human beings is that of "wisdom," virtue, or psychic balance.

On the other hand, the document itself states explicitly that the Psalms call the individual back to "an *essential* religious experience." It does not say that this religious experience is the only one, but it implies that in a balanced religious world it cannot be ignored.

Where does this exegesis of the Psalms lead? The reader will note that in the previous paragraph, moving from the period where action was the key to the religious life of Israel and also was an *essential experience,* we were reminded of the eschatological promise according to which, at the end of history (because it means a *definitive* liberation), God himself will abundantly communicate his Spirit and renew the human heart (see IV,4). So, in the paragraph we are now studying, another emphasis on the present (also outside of time —within the heart, in the existential dimension where the *individual* encounters God, "the Liberator" (IV,4) is added to the emphasis on the hope that awaits us beyond history.

For this same reason, it is interesting to note the double presence of "injustice." As the document states: "Suffering is not purely and simply equated [at least in the Psalms] with the social condition of poverty or . . . political oppression" (IV,5). There is an "also" that points to the major existential problems, such as death, injustice, and failure. It is interesting that among these latter problems we find, explicitly, injustice. Why this duplication, when the suffering that stems from social or political oppression has already been mentioned as something that means the same as injustice? What is the difference?

The difference is, first, in the tool that is applied to the problem. It seems obvious that injustice on the sociopolitical level is fought with sociopolitical tools, through changes introduced into the secular world. But not even the best society can avoid the fact that the individual is faced with existential and personal "injustice" in family life, community life, and so on. It is related to the individual's openness to desires and aspirations that go far beyond available historical instruments. And therefore the "essential religious experience" arises in which God (we could almost say by definition) is the only possible liberator. Such an experience is lived in prayer, and therefore it is not strange that it be reflected particularly in the Psalms. The document criticizes liberation theology for not recognizing the fact that "God, and not man, has the power to change the situations of suffering." The document understands that such a theology places its confidence in liberation from human suffering through historical and secular means.

It is proper to the theology of liberation (at least to that which can be called serious theology) to *unite* these two dimensions: praying and working. Faced with evils that can and should be corrected in history, it does not question the importance of prayer nor substitute enthusiasm for social change for the experience of divine transcendence.

It is also proper for liberation theology to again unite two things that for so long have been separated as if they were antagonistic. The great prophets of Israel pointed the way, and it is one of the "merits" of liberation theology that it has recovered this prophetic relevance (see IX,10). What does the document say about the prophets of the Old Testament? We have already noted that it has taken them out of the context in which they played their decisive role in the religion of Israel. They are rightly characterized as being severely critical of an escapist approach to religion and worship, particularly as related to sociopolitical duties toward the classic categories of the oppressed: the orphans, the widow, the stranger, the worker, and so on. This is so obvious that the document cannot ignore it, although it places the prophets at the end of its review of the Old Testament writings (see IV,6).

The paragraph dedicated to the prophets of Israel, relegated to last place among the Old Testament themes, recognizes the sociopolitical function they exercised in the Lord's name in favor of justice. And it ends by saying, "Justice as regards God and justice as regards mankind are inseparable. God is the defender and the liberator of the poor" (IV,6).

Anyone might read these two sentences as coming from liberation theology, which has so insisted upon them that it seems to have invented them. Can one suppose, then, an approval (even limited) by the Vatican document of these two basic postulates? No, because we must remember the hermeneutical principle utilized in the Introduction: that this document intended only to treat the negative aspects of that theological orientation. Thus the sentences above cannot be taken out of that basic context.

Examined closely, the two sentences represent once more a criticism that we have already found and will continue to find in what follows: liberation theology begins by *separating* the secular from the religious dimension and ends by *reducing* everything to the secular, even the interpretation of the prophetic function in Israel. Thus, according to the document, instead of being directed to *existential* justice, which only God (and not humans) can achieve and offer, liberation theology, by manipulating the prophets, remains in the realm of *secular* justice—what humans want to establish on earth by their own effort and by manipulating social structures.

This, then, is what we find in the inventory reading of the first part of Chapter IV, relating to the Old Testament. Let us now look at what it says about the New.

According to the *Instruction,* what was said in the Old Testament period is "radicalized" in the New Testament. I believe it necessary to suggest (although it may be nothing more than a hypothesis, given what has already been noted) that one must understand such radicalization—in the etymological sense of *going to the root*—in the same sense in which it said that *radical* liberation is *personal* liberation from sin.

If someone asks why the root of things would be more present in the New Testament than in the Old, it seems to me that the answer has much to do with the character of the exegesis that has been done on the latter. The primitive—and overcome—in the Old Testament is a very ambiguous mixture of religious and secular motives. In the New, God becomes more present and religion becomes purer and more interiorized, more properly located *within*—that is, in the heart (IV,7).

To illustrate: the Beatitudes contain the same demands already examined and perceived in the Old Testament. According to the document, they are simply "radicalized" because "conversion and renewal have to occur in the depths of the heart" (IV,7).

To arrive at this conclusion concerning a gospel theme as central as that of the Beatitudes, one must ignore the most scientific and most developed exegesis in Europe and North America—Catholic as well as Protestant. Therefore we have a paradox: the interiorization of the demands for change (attributed to the New Testament in the document) has been made in such a way as to oppose rich and poor, hungry and satisfied, and those who weep and those who laugh (see Lk 6:20-25). Although one cannot ignore the redactional work of Luke (changing all the Beatitudes from the third person to second, as well as the explanatory introduction of the corresponding woes), the redactional work of the author of the first Gospel is even clearer. It is precisely Matthew who *interiorizes* the Beatitudes of Q, adding "of spirit" where the common source said "poor," and "for justice" where he found "hungry."

Obviously, it is not that Matthew says something meaningless, un-Christian, or far from the truth. It is simply that like all New Testament authors, he writes for the instruction of particular Christians. The demands of this context led him to stray occasionally from the more literal memory conserved in the older sources that were closer to the apostolic witness about the meaning of the Beatitudes, historically given by Jesus himself. (It is, of course, difficult to resolve whether these are his own words or whether they represent simply a formula for summarizing Jesus' central attitudes.) It is not that Matthew is mistaken in his interpretation of Jesus as the new Moses, moral lawgiver of the new and definitive Israel. Neither was Matthew unfaithful to Jesus because he converted God's compassion (and that of Jesus) toward the inhuman situation of the most oppressed in Israel into a catalog of moral virtues demanded by this new Lawgiver. But by the same token, it is impossible to ignore the work done regarding the history of the redaction of the synoptics and use nothing but Matthew's version of the Beatitudes as theological proof that the gospel demands must be satisfied only "in the depths of the heart."

In terms of the theology of the document, here—as in the interpretation of the Exodus—there exists in liberation theology a humanistic reductionism which affirms that Yahweh can reveal himself as affected (like any person) by the misery and oppression of the people of Israel as much in the captivity in Egypt as in the Palestine of Jesus' time. The document supposes that God should transcend that type of earthly and secular compassion and has only "religious" motivations in treating and evaluating human situations. Thus, these are treated in their root.

This understanding reappears and is developed even more in the two strangest paragraphs of this biblical chapter: those that refer to poverty and the poor. The first one begins by declaring that in the New Testament "poverty for the sake of the kingdom is praised" (IV,9). I believe it is evident that, the words "for the sake of the kingdom" allude to the poverty that Jesus and his disciples must accept in order to carry out their ministry. To avoid confusion and misunderstandings—because in the synoptics the word "poverty" is not used in this sense—some exegetes rightly prefer to use the word "detachment." And they leave to "poverty" (or the adjective "poor") the negative meaning it has in the Gospel: the inhuman social condition of which many persons and groups are victims. Jesus' not having any place to lay his head does not stem from any lack of what is necessary, which is inflicted upon the individual externally, but rather from the *fullness* of meaning that his internally experienced and embraced vocation implies. The first—the poverty of the poor—dehumanizes; the latter—detachment in pursuit of a historical mission—enriches and humanizes. It is not possible not to perceive the obvious difference that distinguishes both situations, or rather distinguishes the situation and the attitude. The document, although it does not underscore the distinction by using different words, seems to recognize it when it specifies that poverty, evaluated positively in the New Testament, is poverty *for the Kingdom*.

Nevertheless, the document immediately goes from the previous sentence regarding Jesus' detachment to another, this time regarding the poor themselves—those who *suffer* poverty. The reader can judge if this is the case: "Poverty for the sake of the kingdom is praised. And in the figure of the poor, we are led to recognize the mysterious presence of the Son of Man who became poor himself for love for us." (IV,9).[12] This "figure of the poor" is not the figure of Jesus but that of each poor person, because the document tells us that in that figure *we must learn* to "recognize the mysterious presence of the Son of Man."

The document refers, therefore, to every human being who is the victim of poverty; and the proof of this is that it goes on to say that "this is the foundation of the inexhaustible words of Jesus on the judgment in Matthew 25:31-46." This is the primary text for recognizing Jesus, who suffers with the poor, in the poor (*not* in the detached).

But what does poverty "for the sake of the kingdom" have to do with poverty resulting from injustice and oppression? It is clear that they are not the same thing. Possession of the Kingdom is not promised to the poor because of their detachment. According to

Jesus, the poor are not poor for the sake of the Kingdom but *in spite of the Kingdom,* or rather, because it has not yet come.

Any person familiar with the Gospel, and especially with the parable of the last judgment cited by the document itself, will see the relationship between Jesus (poor by acceptance of his vocation) and the poor person (poor by oppressive social conditions). It is not that both suffer the same material want, but that Jesus is hungry every time the least of his brothers and sisters is hungry, and that Jesus is a prisoner every time he or she may be imprisoned. The reason for this "mysterious presence" is not really so mysterious. It is the sympathy or the compassion (they have the same etymological root) that all true love produces, an unlimited love that transmits from the loved one to the lover all that is intolerable and inhuman in the situation he or she suffers.

However, in the document we find (and this is why I said that it seems so strange) a different reason for that affective relationship between the poor and the Son of God. And this reason demonstrates once more how the positive notion of detachment has been unwittingly confused with the negative notion of oppressive poverty: "the mysterious presence of the Son of Man who *became poor himself* for love of us. *This is the foundation of the . . . words of Jesus . . . in Matthew 25:31-46*" (emphasis added). It would seem that the document attempts to say that God is present in the poor not because they are suffering an inhuman situation that strikes at the heart of the one who loves them without limits, but because God sees in their poverty a marvelous quality—the same one that caused the Son of God to come down from heaven to earth. To use the example of the Beatitudes once more, it is as if God were to promise the Kingdom to the poor, not to liberate them from their poverty, but precisely because that poverty contains the divine quality that the Kingdom allegedly embraces and values.

This is the place where the two strangest phrases in the paragraph appear: "Our Lord is one with all in distress; every distress is marked by his presence." It should be made clear that both phrases, in themselves, would be nothing more, in another context, than a passable expression of a correct (although somewhat unusual) interpretation of the message embodied in the parable of the sheep and the goats in the description of the last judgment. In effect, the Judge in that parable shows himself to be one with, and present in, all of his suffering and dehumanized brothers and sisters.

What is so unusual is that the expression in itself, as it is formulated in the document and even more in terms of what preceded it, seems to applaud a positive element in suffering or misery, and this in spite of the fact that it is clear in the parable that the complete opposite is meant. God is truly recognized—for who he is and for what he wants—when the individual is freed from his or her misery. Moreover, if this is not done, no matter how religious one is (see Jas 2:14-17; 1 Jn 4:20), that "mysterious presence" will be replaced by eternal absence: "Out of my sight, you condemned, into that everlasting fire. . . . I was hungry and you gave me no food . . ." (Mt 25:41-42).

That is why it is much more usual in the exegesis of this parable to employ such an expression as "Our Lord is one with the act of *liberation* from all distress; all *humanization* is marked by his presence."[13] And that is why this paragraph in the document is so strange.

It must be repeated, nevertheless, that this strangeness is underlined by what precedes it. In other words, it is marked by an apparent attempt at positively valuing poverty as such, allegedly because God so loved it as to choose it—from among various possible situations—for his Son. In this case, it would appear as if God became poor because poverty possesses a mysterious divine quality. And if this were the case, the primary *religious* attitude toward this poverty would be that of contemplating in it the mysterious presence of Divinity.

That this is the theological intention of the document seems to me undeniable. This is not only because all of the elements already examined point to it, but because further on, and only further on, it speaks, with regard to this same poverty, "of justice and mercy" (IV,10). It says that "at the same time" these "are deepened to assume a new significance in the New Testament": the identification of Christ with everyone who suffers or is persecuted (IV,10). The "at the same time" is a clear sign of a logical separation. In the preceding, then, it spoke of something else; now it is signaling that with it, the need for justice and mercy toward the poor is deepened. Note that that distinction is introduced by the document. It does not exist for the biblical exegete doing liberation theology. What, then, comes *first?* According to the document, what comes logically before the deepening of justice and mercy is the *religious contemplation* of the mysterious presence of God in the poor.

I believe this "deepening" has much to do with "going to the root" of misery and oppression—*sin*. Such "going to the root" prevents us from falling victim to the impatience of struggling against sin's concrete and external manifestations, an impatience that, according to the document, often leads to faith's being captivated by secular ideologies and to the Christian's condoning the use of violent means (see Intro.; II,2-3; IV,7; VII,1-2, and so on).[14]

We thus arrive at the end of the exegetical part of the document. The remaining paragraphs of Chapter IV are only general conclusions. Now I must examine a short paragraph that I have passed over (owing to its general character and not because it lacks value or significance). This paragraph is typical of the theology that grounds the entire document, of that "religious" vision which attempts to adopt what would appear to be God's view of humanity, thus diffusing the conflicts which divide people and make some the victims of others—as the document itself brings to light (see I,4, for example). That is why I believe that it is important to note the tendency in the document to equate all people by using the yardstick of a "religious" notion that allegedly transcends their divisions: "There are no discriminations or limitations which can counter the recognition of *everyone as neighbor*" (IV,8).

This notion is certainly grounded in the Gospel and—as a principle that must precede and preside over the interpretation of the letter of the Law—informs the Lucan parable of the Good Samaritan. But at what point can it be reintroduced, without any historical mediation, in the secular realm as a *law?* That is what the document tries to do: "The commandment of fraternal love extended to all mankind thus provides *the supreme rule* of social life" (ibid.). The Gospel seems, thus, to be used to cause all those who work for the structuring of social life to forget the existence of historical conflicts that divide people. Forgetting this, when so many human sufferings

LIBERATION AND SECULARISM

arise from those conflicts, and making a law out of that "forget-ting," would require a general conversion of hearts to the single sphere where there is no discrimination—*the religious sphere.* There, in effect, is grounded the relativization of all conflict, and there is emphasized the intimate bond that makes all of humanity a fraternal community.

Opposing this "supreme rule of social life" (consisting in a frater-nal love without discrimination), we have the great negative force of society—sin. Thus, "the first liberation, to which all others must make reference, is that from sin" (IV,12). And if it is asked in what way that primacy of liberation from sin is manifested above all other liberations, we are told that it is manifested in the fact that "the New Testament does not require some change in the political or social condition as a prerequisite for entrance into this freedom [brought by Christ]" (IV,13).[15]

As I have already indicated, it would be long and tedious to show that the exegetical quest for the historical Jesus and the commit-ment of his life to the Kingdom does not adopt this position. Further-more, it would be useless because the strength of the argument is not rooted in scientific exegesis but rather in the coherence of a theologi-cal conception that appears cumulatively clearer and with firmer outlines. The document does not hesitate to make a statement that may sound strange so long as it follows directly from the implicitly or explicitly established premises.

From this viewpoint, the general conclusions of the document—derived from the biblical foundations that are treated at the end of Chapter IV—are very important. The first is that there arises "con-sequently" the fact that "the full ambit of sin, *whose first effect is to introduce disorder into the relationship between God and man,* cannot be restricted to 'social sin'" (IV,14).

I repeat emphatically that we would lose sight of the theological importance of such a conclusion if we were to treat it as a caricature of liberation theology. It is true that if one were to ask Latin Ameri-can theologians if they restricted the "ambit of sin" to social sin or even if they localized "evil principally or uniquely in bad social, political, or economic 'structures,'" they would say no. They would add that the insistence upon citing the importance—religious— of the "situation of sin," as Medellín calls it,[16] runs parallel with the opposite tendency in Latin America to privatize religion so that sin is perceived merely as the breaking of a law. Tragically, if no laws are broken—or if their breaking is not visible—Christians do not worry about their complicity in the great evils which society, through its structures, causes to fall upon the most defenseless. The ancient prophets of Israel would say that this is not "to know God." James, in the New Testament, would state that this is not "true religion."

It is true that "social sin" has surprised us by its enormous magnitude as it takes place on a continent that for four centuries—and even today—can be called almost totally Christian. No one pretends that society is the "subject" of that sin. The Christian does not kill (at least not directly) but is an accomplice in millions of deaths that more just social structures could have prevented. But Christians have been taught to identify sin—disorder in one's relationship with God —as that which *directly* has evil as its object. And when an action does not follow a straight line from the one who executes it—or avoids it—to the one who receives its effects, but rather is transmitted through traditional social structures, Christians are accustomed to think that God is not involved and that sin does not exist.

Is this, then, a caricature? It may be, but it is of little importance. Because, looked at closely, what condemns liberation theology is not the phrase "restricted to 'social sin'" but rather that tiny insertion, full of its own kind of theology, that follows the word 'sin': *whose first effect is to introduce disorder into the relationship between God and man.*" If this is true, in the sense in which we have been analyzing this document, the theology of liberation is a deviation from Christian faith. Therefore the exaggeration that may be noted in the criticism that liberation theology "restricts" or "reduces" has little importance; it seems to be enough that it does not make the distinction relating to the "first effect" that is asked for here.

Why, then, would so-called "social" sin not have the effect of introducing disorder between God and the individual as much as "individual" or personal sin? The reason has already been given. For the document, correcting what is called "social sin" is not "a prerequisite for entrance into this freedom" brought by "the grace of

Christ." On the other hand, correcting the disorder between the individual and God in the heart of each person is such a prerequisite.

This is what is stated and explained in the following paragraph. "*Structures,* whether they are good or bad, are the result of man's actions and so *are consequences* more than causes. The root of evil, then, lies in *free and responsible persons* who have to be converted by the grace of Jesus Christ. . . ." (IV,15). Once more we find a distinction that will become a separation: what the *social* has as its object is opposed, first mentally and later in reality, to what the *individual* or *personal* has as its object. The former has, qualitatively speaking, two characteristics: it leads to effects, not to causes, and it is objectively secular, "earthly," "immanentist" (cf. IX,3). The latter, on the contrary, is directed to the causal root and is objectively religious when it sufficiently touches the depths of the person.

From this there arises a most important ulterior consequence: "the search for personal perfection" constitutes the only path to "transcendence" (IV,15). Conversely, to fail to place this accent on personal perfection is the same as "setting out on a road that leads to the denial of the meaning of the person and his transcendence."

Therefore, transcending the limits of the merely human and earthly is a privilege of the transformation of the individual person (also called "conversion of heart"), and cannot be attributed to the (immanent) activities directed at transforming society and its structures. These are not, *of course,* insignificant or worthless but must be conceived of and sought after as stemming from the others. Conversion of heart will necessarily have "effects on the social level." Furthermore, this qualification of being "derived" takes from, or would have to take from, these activities the "pathos" that makes them so defenseless in the face of ideological temptation.

But will that *pathos* not pass to another activity: that of "converting" those "free and responsible persons"? Although this may be the supposed activity of the Church and, as such, that of every Christian, the answer must be in the negative. In effect, as we have already seen in terms of the Psalms, "God and not man has the power to change the situations of suffering" (IV,5). The same thing is said of the "free and responsible persons who have to be converted"; this will be realized "by the grace of Jesus Christ" (IV,15).

Therefore, it would seem, the authentic activity of the individual *becomes*—so as not to say "is bounded by"—the spiritual life of each person, or what the document calls "the search for personal perfection." That appears—unexpectedly—at the end of the paragraph on "social, political or economic structures." Attention is focused on the previously mentioned principles about spiritual life, and then the document speaks of "free and responsible persons who have to be converted by the grace of Jesus Christ." From this conversion comes living and acting "as new creatures in the love of neighbor and in the effective search for justice, *self-control* and the exercise of virtue" (IV,15). The reader may ask what the purpose of self-control is when the document is speaking of "structures which are evil and which cause evil." Well, although it may seem strange to the reader, self-control is the solution proposed for the overthrow of such structures. If there were self-control and the practice of virtue, there would not be unjust social structures. There would be individual injustices which the "effective search for justice" (an undeniable Christian virtue) would put to an end, but there would be no "social sin."

That is the radical deviation from Christian faith that is attributed to liberation theology. The paragraph ends: "To demand first of all a radical revolution in social relations and then to criticize the search for personal perfection is to set out on a road which leads to the denial of the meaning of the person and his transcendence, and to destroy ethics and its foundation which is the character of the distinction between good and evil."[17]

Chapter V, being odd-numbered, does not explicitly contain any negative allusions to the theology of liberation. It is reduced to maintaining (with supporting references) that everything important with respect to liberation is already present in the voice of the magisterium of the Church—beginning with the papal encyclicals, especially those at the time of Vatican II, and ending with the conferences of the Latin American bishops at Medellín and Puebla.

Concerning Chapter VI, all of it is a negative conclusion that has already been cited abundantly. Its basic message is that the theologies of liberation reduce the Gospel to a "purely earthly gospel" (VI,5-6) and, as a result, present a "novel interpretation of the content of faith and of Christian existence which seriously departs from the faith of the Church and, in fact, actually constitutes a practical negation" (VI,9).[18]

Outline and Evaluation

I believe that, after the inventory reading that has just been done (and contrary to what one hoped to see in the document), two important things—extremely important for the entire Church and not only for Latin America—have been manifested.

The *first* is that when the document announces that it *"will be discussing"* (see VI,9), the cause of liberation theology has already been judged. In other words, the decisive criteria for measuring its conformity with Christian faith have been applied and it has been found lacking. I do not mean that the five subsequent chapters, with their constant allusions to Marxism, constitute a mere publicity gimmick to diminish liberation theology in the eyes of those who are not sufficiently sensitive to the profound and subtle methods of theology. I do understand, and I believe I have explained why the devastating force that is attributed to Marxism is not—nor must it have reason to be—based on a profound and nuanced analysis of what Marxism means. It arises, as the document points out, from the fact that when a theology falls from its proper status and is converted into a "purely temporal messianism" (IX,4) or into a "historicist immanentism" (IX,3), accepting its own "absorption into the immanence of history" (X,6), then Marxism today, any Marxism, offers it the means to achieve that messianism deprived of its proper transcendence.

The *second* manifestation is that, although I may have made (like many other theologians in Latin America) a serious effort to discern what positive elements could be taken from Marxism or from other present-day "ideologies," I do not feel that the second half of the document alludes to me. However, I do feel that the theology I have been reading in the first part does allude to me and condemns me. In all sincerity, if the document's theology is correct, and the only one correct, my theology (which I have formulated in my books for almost twenty years and have practiced pastorally) is certainly mistaken.[19]

However, it will be asked: From where does that theology come whose signs we have been finding unmistakeably throughout the first six chapters of the document?

Lay people are often surprised at expressions that are used here in this document for the first time (or for the first time in a long time), and after being accustomed to hearing something very different from religious writers and preachers. Therefore, relying on something which (I believe) cannot a priori be denied, which represents an important theological datum—the consensus of the faithful, the *sensus fidelium*—the layperson asks: but, after Vatican II, weren't we taught something different from what this document contains?

The conclusions of the key texts of Vatican II, and in particular of *Gaudium et Spes* (with the joy of "good news"), have not been lost on the laity, because in twenty years they have learned them. What *is* difficult for the laity—and perhaps for the theologians themselves who do not find these problems substantive—is knowing whether all this opposition between immanence and transcendence, secular and religious, history and the conversion of hearts, and so on and so forth, is anything more than a struggle of and for words. Who actually separates those things? Everyone, utilizing the well-known argument of Aeschines against Demosthenes, rushes to accuse the others of what the others are going to accuse them.

Let us examine this opposition in order to see to what point liberation theology and the theology of the document converge, and at what point they separate, according to the document, irreconcilably.

There are human activities that have as their object introducing changes in history that are humanizing, at least in the intention that gives rise to them. The very concept of history implies that by such activity, *temporal* results are achieved. There are also activities (individual as well as collective, as far as they arise from the heart of each person and have God as their direct object) that introduce modifications in the internal existence of the individual that go beyond the present time; they relate the individual, for good or bad, with the absolute and the eternal.

According to the theology of the document, liberation theology *separates* these two types of activity. This separation allows it to minimize the Absolute and therefore minimize the radical distinction between good and evil (see IV,15). Protected in this way by that separation, Christians who follow the theology of liberation can place all emphasis, and the corresponding *pathos,* on a history where good and evil are subtly and irremediably mixed. Once the importance of the search for personal perfection has been reduced, historical efficacy gives rise to two unacceptable realities. First, there is the expectation that the transformation of economic, social, and political structures will result in the creation of the "new man"—that God alone (not humanity or history manipulated by people) can produce—which thereby reduces the Gospel of salvation to a "purely earthly gospel" (IV,4-5). On the other hand, the very passion for human improvement weakens the discernment of faith,[20] and this results in faith's captivation by systems of supposedly humanizing efficacy: ideologies (see II,2) that propose and employ means which do not respect the person and his or her capacity for transcendence, and thus damage and oppress that person (see VI,2; XI,10).

Let us now hear from the other side. We will use the same schema and begin from the same point. It is a fact that there are human activities that have as their object to introduce humanizing changes into history. These changes appear to be temporal; they are neither cumulative nor irreversible. We see them die every day, just as every person dies, because, like every person, they are subject to corruption and death. But in spite of this, they are the lot of every individual, the field of individual freedom, and the *raison d'être* of each person's uniqueness. There are also activities (individual as well as collective) that, as far as they arise in the heart of each person and have God as their object, relate the individual to the Absolute.

What happens with these *two* types of activity, according to liberation theology? The document, as we have seen, insists that it separates them. But as we have just seen, it is the very theology that we have been reading from the very beginning of the document that separates them: one is utterly transcendent and the other utterly immanent, nothing less. Occasionally, however, the document, forgetting its own harsh dualism, recognizes (or feigns to recognize) that what happens with liberation theology is precisely the exact opposite. "It will be affirmed" (it says, referring to liberation theology) "that *God Himself makes history. It will be added that there is only one history*, one *in which the distinction* between the history of salvation and profane history *is no longer necessary.* . . . There is a tendency to *identify* the kingdom of God and its growth with the human liberation movement" (IX,3; cf. IX,4).[21]

According to the document itself, then, the reason that liberation theology erases the pretended distinction—a distinction that, as such, only the theology of the document establishes, whether or not it is "the" theology of the Church—between the temporal and the eternal, the profane and the sacred, the earthly and the celestial, the history of salvation and the history of human liberation, is nothing other than the *Incarnation* of God.

God makes himself history. Why? Because by becoming one with the lot that every person has *in history* (*Gaudium et Spes,* 22), he converts history, seemingly profane history ("Lord, when did we see you?") into the road by which the individual has access to transcendence and therefore to salvation (*Gaudium et Spes,* 22). Consequently, all people have *only one* vocation, *a divine one* (*Gaudium et Spes,* 22), and they fulfill it insofar as they bring good will and love to the conditions, individual as well as collective, of that one history (*Gaudium et Spes,* 22). Because it does not separate religious history from the profane—without ignoring the singular fact that we are called to live that history with the revelation of the mystery of the individual, hidden by God, within it (*Gaudium et Spes,* 39 and 22)—it is contradictory to accuse liberation theology of "reducing" the Gospel to an earthly gospel. On the contrary, this theology maintains that the eyes of faith illumine this mutual understanding of the earthly city and its history, on the one hand, and the building of the kingdom of God on the other (*Gaudium et Spes,* 40). This is precisely what the most serious exegesis shows us in the conflictive actions of Jesus for the Kingdom.[22] And from that union of both histories that Jesus lived until his death there arises the fact that

Jesus' resurrection carries with it, as the first fruits of the future universal resurrection, not only those persons who have died but also that same "profane" history that seemed subject to corruption. *Everything,* secular and religious, that good will has sown in it will be reaped in the new heaven and the new earth, purified and transfigured (*Gaudium et Spes,* 39). The historical work of all people will lead, by the grace of God, to eschatological metahistory.[23]

This brief enumeration of the principal themes of liberation theology does not pretend to replace much deeper, more nuanced, or more grounded expositions that may be found in abundance. It is only an attempt to show that one must be cautious in pointing out supposed distinctions, separations, and reductions, and in concluding with such an apodictic judgment that the contrary position implies a grave deviation from Christian faith or its practical negation.

Moreover, I believe there is a problem that makes this caution more necessary. For the past twenty years, not only Latin American theologians but also many pastors have carried forward their magisterial and pastoral task in the belief they were following the directives of a much higher magisterium, one with greater authority than that which now says they have seriously deviated. For the same reason, I think this document would have been much more useful for the Church and would have gained greater credibility if those pastors (since it may not have been thought useful to consult with the theologians) had been consulted to discover why they identified with Vatican II (in which many had participated) the theological-pastoral path that they were following. This would have led to a more detailed study to show (or to show with greater clarity) that the theology which appears in the document is compatible with the statements of that higher manifestation of the magisterium—the Council.[24]

Otherwise, Christians would have to think (with understandable logic) that the Holy Spirit, who we believe assisted the Council in the search for and expression of Catholic truth, did not do enough to make the expression clearly understood by the bishops and the faithful, thereby leading those who most wanted to obey the directives of the magisterium to positions that are not only erroneous—

something that may occur in a fallible magisterium—but also heterodox and the practical negation of faith.

I will conclude this evaluation of the document's treatment by citing another important position taken by the pontifical magisterium. In 1965, Paul VI, together with the conciliar fathers, while closing the Second Vatican Council, defended the doctrinal richness of the Council documents—especially the last Constitution to be promulgated, *Gaudium et Spes,* the Pastoral Constitution on the Church in the Modern World. Why do I say "Paul VI defended"? First, because the simple affirmation of the doctrinal richness of *Gaudium et Spes* was directed at those who thought that the Vatican II and in particular *Gaudium et Spes*—being a "pastoral" constitution—lacked dogmatic or doctrinal value. Calling to mind that richness, Paul VI spoke out against the error of thinking that one can effect a profound pastoral renewal without a parallel theological renewal.

But, second, the Pope went on to defend the special doctrinal richness of *Gaudium et Spes* in another way. He foresaw the resistance of a part of the Church and even of some Council fathers to that theology. Moreover, he foresaw the *arguments* that a preconciliar theology was going to use to oppose what already constituted the (apparent) novelty of *Gaudium et Spes*[25]: "Will it not be said that the thought of the Church in Council has deviated toward the *anthropocentric* positions of modern culture?" And when a "that is not the case" might have been expected, the Supreme Pontiff answered his own question (which is, in reality, the question posed by pre-conciliar theology)—"Deviated, no; *turned, yes.*"

This is a clear indication of the difficulty of pre-conciliar theology: it has to change, because the theology of the Council (although it does not condemn errors with canons and anathemas as other councils did) means a turn to an anthropocentric orientation. The temptation will be, therefore, to try to avoid the demanded change and accuse that "turn" toward the most authentic sources of the Christian message of constituting a "deviation" toward the anthropocentric and the earthly.

Paul VI, foreseeing that objection, takes the step of denying precisely the "separation" that this accusation of reductionism implies: "it will have to be recognized that this same concern [by man] *can never be separated* from the more authentic religious concerns, that is, charity, which is the one that gives rise to these concerns (and where there is charity, there is God), due to the *intimate union, constantly affirmed and upheld* by the Council, that exists between *human and temporal values* and properly spiritual, religious, and eternal values. The Church is inclined toward man and *the earth,* but in so doing, raises it toward *the kingdom of God.*" The separation is denied because New Testament exegesis establishes the intimate union that exists between the kingdom of God and "human and temporal values."

But Paul VI goes a step further. The religious has often been identified only with the transcendent dimension of the individual. The Pontiff, summarizing and defending the theology of the Council, returns to the religious its instrumental character: religion, rightly understood, humanizes the person. That is what the discourse proclaims: "Modern mentality, accustomed to judging everything according to its value, that is, according to its usefulness, will have to admit that the value of the Council is great, at least for the following reason: everything in it has been directed toward man's use. May a religion such as the Catholic religion never be declared useless when, in its most conscious and efficacious form, as in the Council, it proclaims religion to be completely at the service of man's good. . . . It gives this explanation of man precisely in virtue of its knowledge of God: to know man, the true man, the complete man, is necessarily to know God."

This closes the circle of that anthropocentric dimension, which is also theocentric, and which cannot be minimized and cannot turn its attention (or its pathos) from the earth and human reality.

This is the authentic and traditional interpretation of Matthew 25:31-46. It is the one that rightly allows the closing of the circle without separation or reductionism: "And if we remember . . . that through the face of each person—especially when tears and suffering have made it more transparent—we can and we must recognize the face of Christ (Mt 25:40), the Son of Man, and if in the face of Christ we can and we must recognize the face of our heavenly Father: 'Whoever sees me,' says Jesus, 'sees the Father' (Jn

14:9), our *humanism* becomes Christian and our Christianity becomes theocentric, in such a way that we can also affirm: *to know God is to know the human person.*"

Where, then, is transcendence? It is not a shortcut from the individual heart to God; it passes through history, where the love of neighbor, made real, is *already* initiated transcendence. That is what conciliar theology meant and why it constitutes a "turn" in the "direction of anthropocentrism." "To teach man to love in order to love God. To love man not as an instrument but as *the first stage toward the highest transcendent stage.*" That is the path to transcendence that is open to the divine vocation that all people of good will follow, according to the theology of the Council.

Here we are faced with the *extraordinary magisterium*[26] of the Catholic Church—an ecumenical council—explained authentically and solemnly by the highest level of the *ordinary magisterium*: the Supreme Pontiff united with the Council fathers.

If Vatican II did not want to condemn errors or those who did not pay attention or follow its teachings, it was not out of carelessness or negligence. As the experience of the Church grows, it knows that often the function of teaching is better accomplished by allowing open discussion than by imposing a particular truth. But this does not exempt important organs of the magisterium, although of lesser authority, from explaining themselves when their theology seems to oppose conciliar teaching. This is especially true when it goes from this—I repeat—"apparent" opposition to the condemnation as heterodox of a theology that, in general, is most literally supported by the teachings of Vatican II and, as such, has been (up until now) allowed and practiced in the Church.

In this way the problematic has changed somewhat since my initial statements. It is no longer an issue of how to join the respect owed to the ordinary magisterium of the Church of Christ with the sincere search that the very existence of that same magisterium (saying and knowing that it is fallible) implies. The problem has now become both easier and more difficult to solve: it entails the fact that there is no visible continuity between different expressions of the ordinary magisterium.

The solution is easier because there are different grades of authority within the ordinary magisterium, and fidelity to it not only can but must take into account such differences. But the solution is also more difficult because the difference between distinct expressions of the ordinary magisterium can be such that the option for one, although it may be backed by the authority of an ecumenical Council and the Sovereign Pontiff (who presided during many of its sessions and closed it), may mean opposition to another.

What is that opposition? Of course, it is not incumbent upon me to ask an accounting of a Congregation, charged by the Holy Father to oversee the Doctrine of the Faith, about how it understands its relationship with the "doctrinal richness" of Vatican II. In my view, the document coming from that Congregation has not yet presented proof that the theology of liberation, in its most basic, fundamental, and universally known characteristics, is a "serious deviation from Christian faith," much less that it is "its practical negation." I may be told that the document has no reason to present that proof and that it is sufficient merely to proclaim such a condemnation. Again, I must say with all sincerity that I do not believe this, and precisely because—beyond any other reason—the document itself has stated with all sincerity, as has been seen in the preceding pages, what it understands as the proof of what it has affirmed.

EXCURSUS

The Beginning of Faith: The History of a Small Idea

The fact that I have from the beginning been linked in friendship and in work to the group of Latin American theologians who began to think and act in accord with what today is called the theology of liberation allows me to clarify some historical-theological points that perhaps may go a little further than the purely anecdotal. I hope that what I am going to discuss here, by way of an appendix to this chapter, will help the reader form a more fitting conception of some lines of thought that influenced the origins of that theology and today influence the disqualification made by the document studied here.

My testimony is, in this case, personal. As I experienced the birth of a new Latin American theology, it was something like the spontaneous generation of a common thought arising in isolation in various parts of the continent. Only when various Latin American (by birth or by adoption) theologians began to meet and share the views of one another did we begin to perceive similarities and convergences.

I would like to show how a particular and small theological idea had its specific contribution in that formation of liberation theology, how that idea came to be universalized through Vatican II (and especially in *Gaudium et Spes*), and how that same idea today is perhaps the deepest and most centrally attacked by the theology that appears in the recent Vatican document.

I insist that this is a *personal* testimony of the origins of liberation theology in order to correct two mistakes. I am speaking of 1960, when Vatican II had not yet been convoked and when none of us could have foreseen *Gaudium et Spes*. Hence it is not true that the origin of that theology must have been situated in Vatican II. And it does not mean to claim any special originality, but rather to appreciate the common elements as well as the differences between *Gaudium et Spes* and Medellín, for example, as well as between the theology of the Council and liberation theology.

Second, what each of us brought as contributions to the common task was the theological traditions stemming from our respective studies. Practically all of us had completed them in European schools. This may give rise to criticism (which I do not wish to discuss here so as not to stray from the purpose of these pages). There is no reason to be embarassed about this European origin (although, for chronological reasons, political theology does not figure in it, as some imagine). Liberation theology did not arise out of the jungle or out of a vacuum; neither did its related popular movements or communities. Furthermore, I believe that the European theology of that time—like that of the Council—contained elements proper to the context from which it emerged as well as important elements common to the Christian faith which, united to our Latin American experience, would have us take new and often unexpected directions.

Each one of us was influenced in a different way and (at least in my case) in isolation by the theology studied in Europe. Of those who had been my companions in theology, I had been a friend only of Gustavo Gutiérrez while he was studying theology in Lyons—a friendship of a lifetime.

In 1953 I began my second year of theology (after having completed the first year in Argentina) at Eegenhoven, Louvain, in Belgium. There I attended the course on the theology of grace given by an excellent theologian, Leopold Malevez. His shyness always kept him in the background. I have to thank him, first, for a certainly undeserved friendship for a mere student who was furthermore a foreigner. On the intellectual and theological level, what I have always understood as my own "theology of liberation" began with him—a theology I amplified once I had returned to Latin America.

During those years, it was commonly taught in Catholic theology that the grace of God lifted the individual to a *supernatural plane,* beginning with the acceptance of faith (and consequent baptism). Before that, the person moved on a level where, it was supposed, the destiny and efficacy of human actions led only to *natural* and temporal ends. One's intimate relationship with God and heavenly destiny *began with faith,* a gift from God which inaugurated that habitual gift of the supernatural.[27]

Malevez reminded us, however, that in view of this conception, a theologically important Council, the second of Orange (529), had intervened in the dispute between the disciples of Augustine and those of Pelagius (the semi-Pelagians) to declare that the "beginning of faith," or rather, the preparation for it, was *already supernatural.*

In effect, no one truly can be prepared for something that absolutely is above him or her, something that by definition is beyond the individual's possibilities and destiny. Therefore, this declaration of the Council of Orange on the *initium fidei* was known by theology (at least until the end of the Middle Ages), and it was not extraordinary to speak of the supernatural character of the beginning of faith.

The novelty of Malevez's position was that, based on historical reasons, the "preparation of faith" was not reduced (as it was with Rahner for a time) to the situation in which a person, faced with the Christian message, begins to feel attracted by it and acts accordingly, gradually becoming informed about the Christian faith, meditating on it, and so on. Malevez reminded us of the historical context of the controversy. What in reality concerned the participants in that discussion, under the title "the beginning of faith," was the *human virtues* that the pagan world of antiquity seemed to exhibit. The Fathers (Eusebius of Caesarea, for example, cited by *Lumen Gentium,* 16) had already spoken, in view of such virtues, of a "preparation for the Gospel." For virtuous persons and, in some way more generally, for the entire long march of human good will in history, there must be the understanding that no one is prepared or begins something that totally exceeds his or her possibilities.

Thus, when the Council of Orange declared that the "beginning of faith" was already supernatural, it was stating that the entire road traveled by the pagans (guided by good will and love)—toward the God who is love and toward the Christian message of that Mystery hidden in love—was already (even though it did not lead to the faith) from God, from freely-given grace, and related to the plane of supernatural efficacy.

With this, Malevez anticipated[28] what Karl Rahner, from a more speculative point of view, baptized with a term that had wide currency and acceptance: *the supernatural existential.* This term said, in reality, the same thing expressed by Malevez, although it gave it more explicitly the universal dimensions that corresponded to it. Although the intimate relationship with God and with heaven may not belong to *human nature,* no real human existence developed on a purely natural plane. From the beginning of humanity, God's grace placed all persons on the path toward the intimate relationship with him and with celestial life.

It is important to point out that ten years after I first received the theological foundation for a completely universal and human vision of God's grace, the *Dogmatic* Constitution On The Church (*Lumen Gentium*) reiterated what was affirmed by the Council of Orange—

declaring that the Church considers as "a preparation for the Gospel" everything good and true that is found among people who have lived according to their highest potential and in accord with their conscience—even without arriving at explicit knowledge of God. Whoever says "preparation," using the same principle as Orange, places the one who is prepared and that which is being prepared for on the same level of salvation (see LG 16).

Moreover, it could be said that in *Lumen Gentium* this great theological principle, although accepted, is minimized by the fact that the interest of the Constitution is the Church, still conceived in the traditional way as a "perfect society." Although the Constitution serves the aims of ecumenism, it does not reach as far as *Gaudium et Spes,* which summarizes the conciliar vision, as Paul VI says, of turning to God to know man, and to man to know God.

In effect, this principle is the theological category that destroys the compartmentalization of the profane and the sacred, of the natural and the supernatural.[29] Owing to the recovered unity, the Church can now respect and embrace "the joy and hope, the grief and anguish" (*Gaudium et Spes,* 1) of humanity and "become," as Paul VI says, "anthropocentric" without ceasing to be authentically "theocentric."

If, in spite of this, there is a particular difference between the Latin American theology of liberation and conciliar theology, it is not because the former reduces the gospel of salvation to a merely human and earthly gospel any more than the latter does. From that point of view, there is little difference between the one and the other, just as the Council and Medellín more or less coincide even though they do not say the same thing nor use the same language.

Indeed, the difference that does exist is visible, and that context led to the need for a Medellín three years after *Gaudium et Spes.* A Council, no matter how ecumenical it may be, will always be "situated" by the influences that prevail within it. And although Rahner's influence, for example, may have opened up a universally valid road, Rahner himself saw it from a viewpoint proper to the more developed European countries. We may take as an example the discourse of Paul VI cited earlier. There we find two clear references to this context of problems: "anthropocentric direction of modern

culture," "modern mentality." Now, that "coming of age" of which
Bonhoeffer speaks, and that the Holy Father more prudently refers
to as "modernity," confronts the problems proper to the progress of
a secular world, ambiguous in its realizations and its future. Citizens
of developed nations often do not know what to do or where to direct
the results of technical discoveries and "successes."[30]

The Latin American, however slightly noticed, faces a very different problematic, and it is logical that our theology (as identified as it
may be with the tenor of *Gaudium et Spes*) is inclined toward such a
problematic. It is uniquely real on our continent.

The fact that the need to rethink it in and for Latin America was
felt only three years after the Council is itself very eloquent and has
no parallel with the reception of the Council in other continents or
geographical or cultural contexts. This is why, in 1968, the Latin
American bishops gathered in Medellín to "adapt" the directives of
Vatican II to the reality of the continent.

This need did not stem from the fact that a "theology of liberation" existed in Latin America. It arose from the fact that the
situation was unlike that of developed nations. The problem was
simply what to do with people who had been trampled upon, humili-
ated, and deformed by centuries of oppression and suffering.

Therefore, even in this first stage, one could say—committing a
small anachronism—that Latin American "liberation theology"
already existed at the time of the Council, and developed out of the
same forces that characterized the "anthropocentric shift" that also
distinguishes post-conciliar North Atlantic theology. I simply point
out that this shift affects universal Catholic theology and is therefore equally condemnable as reductionist and secularizing by the
theology present in the *Instruction* from the Congregation for the
Doctrine of the Faith.

This implicit and wider dimension of the condemnation can be
seen in the summary published by *Osservatore Romano* of an interview with Cardinal Ratzinger concerning a kind of appraisal of the
twenty years since the Council.[31]

In this "appraisal" there reappears the initial idea (which I
received from Leopold Malevez) of one history wherein all good will
throughout the ages is led by the grace of God to the final and

salvific encounter with Jesus Christ. This idea, like liberation theology in which it has one of its most secure and traditional basis, is criticized by Cardinal Ratzinger as one of the most unfortunate elements of this post-conciliar period.

He says, speaking in general, "It is true that the results seem cruelly opposed to everyone's expectations, beginning with those of John XXIII and later Paul VI. . . . One expected a new enthusiasm and many have ended in discouragement and boredom. . . . The appraisal seems, then, negative; I repeat what I said ten years after the end of the Council's work: It is unquestionable that this period has been decidedly unfavorable to the Catholic Church."

Before passing from the general to the particular point that concerns us, I believe it necessary to point out an element in this global judgment relevant to *all* theology. The reader is certain to see that the interpretation of a summary of a conversation always runs the risk of deforming the thought being interpreted. But since the Cardinal permitted its publication in this form, one must presume that he approved of its wording.

This global judgment is certainly disconcerting, at least at first glance. It is true that, in one way or another, the majority of Christians committed to their faith were bewildered after the Council. But is it licit to unite under one judgment two opposite kinds of discontent: one that stems from the fact that the Council or the post-Council age has gone too far, and the one other, from the fact that the post-conciliar Church may have abandoned too soon the achievement of conciliar thought and not gone far enough?

On the other hand, the Cardinal points to a hoped-for and a frustrated result: "One expected a new enthusiasm and many have ended in discouragement and boredom." From every point of view, it is impossible to recognize boredom and discouragement in the reality of the Latin American Church. Where Christianity means concrete commitment, accepted dangers, and prophecy (with everything that, according to the Gospel, is the terrible consequence of the prophet's fate), discouragement may momentarily overshadow enthusiasm. But boredom, no! Therefore I believe that this observation is important for understanding the negativity of post-conciliar phenomena: boredom seems clearly to mean immobility or paralysis. It is not usually the result of "going too far."

However, returning to the interview, an important question arises in view of the negative picture painted there: is what happened after the Council due to the Council itself, or to what happened afterwards—or to both factors? Cardinal Ratzinger's answer deserves attention for how curious and unnuanced it is: "I have the impression that the imperfections that have been found *inside* the Church during these twenty years are owed more to the unleashing of latent, aggressive, polemical, centrifugal, and perhaps irresponsible forces than to the 'true' Council; and—*outside* the Church—to the impact of cultural change: the affirmation in the west of an upper middle-class, of the new 'tertiary bourgeoisie' with its liberal-radical ideology of individualism, rationalism, and hedonism." Going to the core of our question, or rather to the specific responsibility of the Council for this state of affairs, and supposing (as it is necessary to suppose) the normal care for language proper to a theologian and member of the hierarchy, it is important to note that the Cardinal splits the negative responsibilities. The *majority* of them are owed to factors that are unchained as much within as outside the Church and thereby have caused a displacement between the Council and its realization. The *minority* of them are owed to the Council itself. If this were not the case, it would have been much more natural to employ the simplest and most helpful phrase: *not this, but that.* But what he says is: *More* to this *than* to that.[32]

Among the conciliar points that have been exaggerated or have deviated, whether within the Council itself or after it, according to this same interview, are two that are intimately related to the idea regarding the beginning of faith. The two titles beneath which these points are discussed will be significant to the reader: "The values of others" and "Church-world relationship."

In the first case, he says: "Beginning with the years of the Council, the traditional doctrine of the Church that every person is called to salvation and in fact can save him or her self even if he or she may not be a visible member of the Catholic community has been excessively emphasized. . . . 'Among other things, the link that the New

Testament establishes between salvation and truth has been forgotten, a link (Jesus affirmed it explicitly) that liberates and, as such, saves.'"[33]

I understand that, in spite of its appearance to the contrary, this statement does not allude to subsequent deformations but to an exaggeration of the Council itself, of having forgotten something, more probably of *Gaudium et Spes's* treatment of the subject. This Constitution, after describing the "Christian" who arrives, "united to the paschal mystery" at the resurrection, adds without any attempt at continuity: "*All this holds true not for Christians only but also for all men of good will* in whose hearts *grace is active* invisibly. For since Christ died for all, and since all men are in fact called to *one and the same destiny, which is divine, we must hold* that the Holy Spirit offers to all the possibility of being made partners, in a way known to God, in the paschal mystery" (*Gaudium et Spes,* 22).

I confess that it does not seem possible to me to "excessively emphasize" this principle. Moreover, and at the risk of appearing childish (at sixty years of age), I confess that, twenty years after Vatican II, I feel the same enthusiasm that I felt then at this "doctrinal richness," a richness that is still far from reaching and illuminating the whole Church. I admit that I may be mistaken. But, with so simple and clear a statement, this error—which would cause me to overemphasize the universality of grace and salvation—would have to be attributed to the very doctrine of the Council. Presumably the Council, by making such a statement, would have forgotten certain preconditions (like 1 Timothy 2:4-7) that would limit the extension of that principle. In any case, it could not be attributed to postconciliar exaggerations.

There is, furthermore, something here that seems easy to resolve. Rightly, Cardinal Ratzinger, alluding to this conciliar principle, calls it "the traditional doctrine of the Church." But the reader has to be an expert in theology to know in what strict sense this doctrine was traditional at the time the Council proclaimed it so. Otherwise, he or she might erroneously take the word in its obvious meaning, and assume that *Gaudium et Spes* had been merely repeating a doctrine known and accepted for some time. And this would logically lead to thinking that those who wanted to lead the Church to the consequences of that principle (as if it were a new one) would have been "polemical" or even "irresponsible" innovators.

The technical sense of the word "traditional" does not imply that a doctrine may or may not be accepted at a given time but rather its fundamental accord with the source of Christian faith—God's revelation. Only in that sense was the scope of salvation, as expressed by Vatican II, *traditional.*

The proof of this is that when theology was taught in thesis form (and the theses had to be sent to Rome for approval), Leopold Malevez never dared to make this idea as central as we are doing here. Neither must one forget that Karl Rahner, at the same time that he began to intervene so decisively in the Council, was prohibited from publishing what he had written without submitting it to the Vatican censors. His attempt at opening the idea of the "Mystical Body" (as Pius XII conceived it in *Mystici Corporis*) to embrace non-Christians of good will meant he had to write an article of almost one hundred pages in approval of the Encyclical to be able to say in the final two or three pages what was his true thesis (as can be seen in the second volume of his *Theological Investigations*).

The Council itself only began to uncover some of the consequences of that "traditional doctrine" on "the values of others" (see, for example, *Gaudium et Spes,* 44). Witness to this is the discovery that atheism can be the fruit of a person's good will colliding with a deformed and irreconcilable image of God (*Gaudium et Spes,* 19). And the consequent solemn commitment of the Church to seriously study the profound causes of atheism (*Gaudium et Spes,* 21) is a commitment that remains unfulfilled, above all in recent times. The *Instruction* nevertheless supposes (without recalling Vatican II) that "atheism and the denial of the human person, his liberty and his rights" constitutes the core of the conception of all Marxist truth (VII,9) and therefore the goal of all its tangible efforts.

Therefore, because the doctrine was not "traditional" in the ordinary sense of the word, the scope of grace and salvation produced the crisis to which Cardinal Ratzinger accurately alludes when he points out that many, after the Council, began to ask themselves:

"Why bother the non-Christians, inducing them to baptism and to faith in Christ, since their religion is the road to salvation in their culture, in their part of the world?" But it is also true that missiology was renewed through this crisis. New roads and new forms of carrying the Gospel of Jesus Christ were opened. A Synod established that the struggle for justice—a task that is far from ending and certainly not "boring"—was an *integral part* of evangelization. Paul VI exhorted the bishops of Africa to carry out, after an initial evangelization very much tied to colonialism, the true inculturation of Christianity in indigenous cultures—a task that is still far from being done and one that has been stopped too soon. In any event, there is nothing that is less likely to give rise to discouragement and boredom.

I will not spend too much time on the second previously mentioned point: the Church-world relationship. The reader will immediately relate this subject to Malevez's idea, since it determines what there is to see in the "world"—secular in appearance—with the eyes of Christian faith.

To this end, Cardinal Ratzinger says in his interview:

> Vatican II was right in desiring a renewal of the relations between the Church and the world. Nevertheless, neither the Church nor the world is known by anyone who thinks that these two realities can meet without conflict or even may be mixed. Even more so, today as never before, the Christian must be conscious of belonging to a minority and of being opposed to what appears good, obvious, and logical to the "spirit of the world," as the New Testament calls it. Among the more urgent tasks of the Christian is the recovery of the ability to oppose many of the tendencies of the culture that surrounds him, renouncing an excessively euphoric, post-conciliar solidarity.

As far as the description and evaluation, positive or negative, with its "more or less," of the modern world, the Council was logically the product of its day and its context. In light of the previous discussion —showing the contextual differences between Latin American liberation theology and the dominant theology of Vatican II—I believe that the majority of theologians in Latin America will agree with Cardinal Ratzinger that the Council was too optimistic in its vision or expectations regarding the values of this world. It is a matter of pastoral prudence, and perhaps the Fathers of the Council could not perceive in their description of the world certain aspects of global reality that were developing such as "in the west a middle upper-class, of the new 'tertiary bourgeosie.' "

But in terms of the *theology* about the Church and its relationship to the world, I believe that the paragraph analyzed here would disorient many Christians if Cardinal Ratzinger himself had not given the key to understanding it correctly. This key consists in perceiving that "world" is used, as in the Fourth Gospel, in two different senses: first, as the dwelling of humans—therefore, as representing the entire human family—and second, as a negative principle, "the spirit of the world"—allegedly in opposition to the harsh demands of the authenticity and truth of the life, struggle, and message of Jesus.

Nevertheless, the fact that this key is not explained as such causes the principles about the Church-world relationships to appear (in the same way as in liberation theology) as opposed to the theology of Vatican II (and not as mere superficial distortions). Thus, for example, why can "these two realities" not be "mixed," since the Council itself expounded its theology to call Christians, "as citizens of both cities," and to point out that the Church "travels the same journey as all mankind and shares the same earthly lot with the world," and, finally, to declare that it is faith that opens to us the mystery that "the earthly and the heavenly city penetrate one another" (*Gaudium et Spes*, 40-43).

And again here at the crossroads there returns the small "traditional" idea about the interpretation of the Council of Orange on the supernatural value of the beginning of faith. That is because this interpretation, and only this one, prevents thinking of the history of the world and of the Church, the history of human effort and that of grace and salvation, as two floors in the same building.

There is something strange in the insistence on the opposition of Church and world. What is the Church but a part of the world? Not only sociologically but theologically as well. The Council confirms this, understanding "world" as a synonym for "the whole human family" to which the "People of God [identified here with the Church] belongs" (*Gaudium et Spes,* 3).

If that "People" has a specific character, is it not that of possessing grace? The Council, following the same idea that I am developing here, answers *no* (see *Gaudium et Spes,* 22). It does answer that the Church is distinct because the mystery of humankind and our divine vocation have been made clear to the faithful. Then how does one separate the Church from the world if the members of the former, exactly as the members of the latter, must react critically and firmly against the "spirit of the world"? Perhaps one thinks that the people "of the world" necessarily follow "the spirit of the world"—individualism, rationalism, hedonism—and that, in spite of this, are called to good will and march toward faith and salvation. This is not what the Council says theologically, despite how optimistic it may seem in terms of the good will of the world in general. And much less does liberation theology say it.

* * *

The reader will have to excuse this parenthesis—perhaps too laden with personal memories that cover the last thirty years. What is presented here supports what I have tried to explain, albeit negatively, in the preceding chapter.

3

LIBERATION AND HERMENEUTICS

Why does the document on liberation theology continue, since it has already demonstrated its basic theological argument—secular reductionism—in proof that such theology is unorthodox?

The first step—properly theological—has already been taken. And what was essential for discerning the orthodoxy or heterodoxy of Latin American theology (and by extension, that of North Atlantic countries insofar as it has followed most closely the teachings of Vatican II) has already been set forth.

To a certain degree, what follows is not "theological," at least not directly so. It is something like a *demonstration of effects*. Chapters VII-XI of the document try to make the so-called reductionism of liberation theology still more manifest—if that is possible. But this is done in such a way that it is no longer possible to apply these chapters to the greater part of European or North Atlantic theology. Hence the majority of North Atlantic theologians may be able to read these chapters as something far removed from them and as something that does not speak to them.[1]

It has already been indicated that there is a vast difference in human *context*. Vatican II, tributary of a renewal of European theology, wanted to dialogue with the contemporary world, with what Paul VI calls the modern culture or "modernity." But the spokesperson for these characteristics, the one who was actually present at the Council, was the developed human being of the West, laden with the problems of developed nations.

The interlocutor of Latin American theology, the one who was present at Medellín, is again the human being. But it is a different person: dehumanized and oppressed, not only (or not so much) by happenstance or by the abuse of persons or particular groups, but systematically through the economic, social, and political mechanisms that perpetuate and, as the document studied here definitely points out, support one another by enlarging and consolidating their destructive work (see I,2).

It is to this, and not to the developed and presumably "mature" human being, that one must speak of God, of God's plan, of pain and sin. This means an important difference in context; but there is something more. One could almost say that the very notion of context changes. One is no longer speaking of *circum*-stances, which are all around, but of something more decisive and closer to the most delicate core of the human being where all the value and meaning of the human person are put into play.

The reader should remember that in the previous chapter the discourse of Paul VI was cited: to know man, one needs to know God, and to know God is to know man. The order of the two phrases is of little importance, because what is established is a hermeneutical *circle*. If there were a first and a second in irreversible order, one could not say that the knowledge of the latter conditions that of the former.

Let us take an example from the previous chapter. The document attempted to be a negative criticism of liberation theology: all human liberation had to have reference to the radical, or primary, liberation—"liberation from sin" (IV,12; see Introduction; IV,2; and so on)—understanding it as "the disorder of the relationship between man and God"(IV,14). The document seems to suppose that it is now clear what must be the basis and the root for the creation of the "new man." Nevertheless, the problem is more complicated if the words of Paul VI about knowing man in order to know God are to be taken seriously. This logically implies that the knowledge of the human condition should be present in order to understand what we should call order or disorder in the relationship between humankind and God, and only then can we know what is truly sinful.

This, and nothing else, is what liberation theology tries to do in the particular context mentioned here. According to the document, liberation theology does not want to admit that radical liberation is liberation from sin. In reality, not one of us—including all the theologians who can be considered liberation theologians whom I know in Latin America—ever hesitated to admit that radical liberation is liberation from sin.

What liberation theology does deny (in agreement with Paul VI's closing remarks at Vatican II) is a type of hermeneutical innocence according to which it is enough merely to cite "sin" or "right relationship between God and man," in order to interpret concrete reality or the Bible itself as the word of God.

Perhaps this may be seen more clearly by quoting the document: "Nor can one localize evil principally or uniquely in bad social, political or economic 'structures' as though all other evils came from them *so that the creation of the 'new man' would depend on the establishment of different economic and socio-political structures*" (IV,15). "Principally or uniquely" appears only in the first part of the sentence. Grammatically speaking, the second part should be read as if the creation of the "new man" *did not depend* on the establishment of new social structures. But that "new man" will think and express himself, logically, according to what he is—in a new way. No one can ignore how language and, therefore, thought itself depends on culture, which *is* an economic-sociopolitical structure.

Originally, for example, the words "villager," in older usage, and "bourgeois," in Western modern languages, both signified a socio-geographical designation (the inhabitants of villages or burgs, as opposed to the inhabitants of castles or mansions). The ties between that geographical "place" and the corresponding economic, social, and political "place" cause both words to be used more and more to designate social classes. Finally, the struggle or conflict between those classes, added to the "linguistic" power of those "structures" of society, made both words become pejoratives.

A similar slip of language between "poor" and "sinners," on the part of the Pharisees and religious authorities of Israel, is visible in the Gospel (compare Mt 5:3 and 11:5 with 9:11 and 11:19). What is behind this linguistic slip obligates Jesus to create a long series of parables, destined to tear down the linguistic barrier that made impossible the hope of the poor for a kingdom meant for them. Showing who the true "sinners" were in Israel (cf. Lk 15:25-32; 18:9-14; Mt 18:23; 20:1-47; 21:28-36, and so on), Jesus shows how the radical liberation from sin is itself conditioned by the recognition of that sin, which is in turn conditioned by one of the deepest social structures—the one that generates a type of language that makes the individual insensitive as much to the (hermeneutical) interpretation of the signs of the times as to the interpretation of the word of God about sin.

Why could Jesus not point directly to the root—that is to say, to the sin that introduced disorder into the relationship between God and humankind? For the same reason we cannot do it in Latin America— because the structures of society in Israel had denaturalized (semantically) what was meant by "sin." Thus, to go to the root, and not to escape from it, it was necessary to reinstitute the authentic conception of the true relationship between the person and God in the particular sphere where language is created. Otherwise, would it have been possible to change a concept of sin rooted in the most powerful social interests in israel? Or could Jesus' "new man" speak an "old" language?

Therefore the *radicality* of sin does not lie in its *independence* from any social conditioning. This hermeneutical circle, although understood or emphasized differently by diverse groups, is proper to liberation theology in Latin America.[2]

This certainly is not in opposition to post-conciliar European theology, which also must admit it. But, as we have seen, the problems are different. European (or if one prefers, North Atlantic) theology points more toward the uncertain and dangerous future of *developed* humanity. Latin American theology, turned more toward an inhuman past staunchly defended by structures of every kind (including religious ones), has to pose different questions.

This hermeneutical circularity, the consequence of the theology outlined above, places a question mark on that double task, which the document seems to conceive as a clear and easy function of faith: to discern the signs of the times through an analysis of the reality that may be totally docile to it, and to respect the discernment imposed by the word of God as found in the Bible. The chapters we must now study precisely treat the deviations in these two fields: "Concepts uncritically borrowed from Marxist ideology and recourse to theses of a biblical hermeneutic marked by rationalism are at the basis of the new interpretation . . ."(VI,10).

We must here add a simplifying and clarifying note to this introduction to the second part of the document.

I believe it is clear, whether or not the principle is accepted, that in post-conciliar Catholic theology the need for a circular or spiral hermeneutic has been called for: to know God it is necessary to know humankind, and vice versa. And the same is true for loving him.

It is not for merely utilitarian and apologetic reasons that post-conciliar theology seeks to enter into dialogue with the existing, contemporary, human problems. And the problems themselves vary from region to region.[3] In the societies on the outskirts of the large developed centers, the basic human problem, the one that urges and impassions, is (as the document itself affirms) the one that relates to *justice*.

It is not strange then that the ideology (mistaken or not) which since the last century has made its center the search for more just structures should appear beside a theology that must move toward God by passing through the reality of a people subjected to terrible injustices. There is an undeniable affinity between the vision demanded by the Christian message in Latin American and any analysis that concentrates on explaining the injustice suffered by the people.

But, it will be asked, what does *rationalism* have to do with the interpretation of the word of God in the Bible? The hermeneutical circle is also valid for the Bible. If it gives us without further ado the right knowledge of God, the principle that to know God it is necessary to know humankind would be meaningless. And vice versa: if it is through a critical relationship with justice that we know the dehumanized and oppressed of our continent, it is also with our eye on that justice that we hear and understand the word that God speaks to us in the Bible.

That is why I say that it is one and the same negative judgment that is being applied both to the reality and the biblical exegesis that are proper to liberation theology. The "rationalistic hermeneutic of revelation" is (as was seen in Chapter IV and will be seen again in X) nothing other than certain elements of Marxism applied to the interpretation of the Bible, with its logical consequences, according

to the document: relativization, class conflict, political reductionism, and so on.

Posing the Question

After that summary, which I believe clarifies the entire second part
of the document by introducing the single question of method, I will
begin with some theological considerations.

It could be objected that the logical procedure would be a inventory
reading, (this time of Chapters VII-XI), as we did with the first part
of the document. But there are two reasons against that.

The first is *practical*. Even though the chapters of the first part
offered a clear and logical order, those of the second part are a
strange melange. Except for the recurring principal theme, it is not
easy to find one's way in terms of a logical development from one
thing to another. One has the impression of facing a potpourri of all
the points—this time much more specific and therefore perhaps
more difficult to unify—in which the orientations of the Vatican
(and not always for reasons of theological orthodoxy) discern something negative in Latin American theology as well as in its pastoral
activity.

The second reason is more *theoretical*. And it consists in repeating something that I consider to be indispensable for the understanding and theological judgment of the document: the verdict about the
theology of liberation is already handed down *at the beginning* of
this second part. Even if Marxism did not exist—and today many of
the most famous theologians in Latin America have nothing more
than a polite relationship with Marxism—liberation theology would
be condemned as a humanistic, earthly, and secular reduction of the
Gospel of salvation.

Therefore, before beginning a critical reading we must ask: what
is the theological status of this second part? As will be seen later, I
believe that the vast majority of the elements for judging this question are found in Chapter VII.

I begin, then, from the fact that the reader knows vaguely, from
the introduction to this paragraph, that the second part of the document (and even supposedly all of it) will speak about the specific

relationship of liberation theology to distinct elements of Marxism (or, as the document often calls it, "Marxist ideology"). However, what at first glance would appear to be a clear proposition is not, because, if it is true that in Chapters I-VI we have a fairly precise description of what the document means by liberation theology, that is not true of the second term, "Marxism."

This imprecision is important. Because, if in such a short time—as the document recognizes—there are already various theologies of liberation, there must be ten times as many Marxisms, if for no other reason than the age difference between the two currents of thought. The document, although it does not quantify this disproportion, does admit that "Marxist thought even since its origins, and even more so lately, has become divided and has given birth to various currents which diverge significantly from one another"(VII,8).

Given that situation, let us examine all the elements that the document proffers (above all in this crucial Chapter VII) for understanding Marxism—or rather, the way in which the document faces or conceives it. But let us not lose sight of the theological question that concerns us most deeply: what is the theological status of this teaching of the magisterium about the relationship of Marxism to theology?

I believe that by beginning in this manner we will find several interesting points. *First,* as has already been seen, it says the same thing about Marxism that it does about liberation theology: there is not one but many. But, on the surface at least, it does not come to the same conclusions. Or rather, it does not take the same precaution of speaking of Marxisms in the plural.

There is no direct answer in the document as to why this is so. Without it, we can only presume what could have been the reason for not taking the same course. I believe it is safe to suppose the following. I indicated in the previous chapter that, from my point of view, no true liberation theology escaped the criticism made by the document, at least what is commonly understood as theology and not the vague aspiration described in Chapter I of the document. Nevertheless, it cannot (and in fact does not want to) deny the *theoretical possibility* of a correct theology of liberation—among other reasons, I suppose, because it is a subject coming out of the pontifical teachings themselves. Furthermore, the document demonstrates what would be the basis—in the Bible as well as in the magisterium—of that correct theology. That is why one paragraph (on the pluralism of theologies of liberation) follows another where the implicit reason is clearly explained: "We noted above that an authentic theology of liberation will be one which is rooted in the Word of God, correctly interpreted [by the magisterium]"(VI,7).

This intention is not applicable to the use of the plural in the case of Marxism. The document does not indicate that, despite differences, there exists an acceptable Marxism. The mention of the internal differences within Marxism seems here more a warning so that no one will fall into the temptation of using this variety in order to excuse themselves for "borrowing" some elements from some Marxist authors on the grounds that—since not all Marxists agree— they can be removed from the system and presented as, say, non-Marxists, or even as independent of Marxism.

That is the precise reason why the mention of what could be called *different Marxisms* is preceded by two paragraphs in which it is shown that the internal force of Marxism is such that one cannot take a single element from it without "having to accept the entire ideology" (VII,6), that is, the entire system as well as "the kind of totalitarian society to which this process slowly leads" (VII,7).[4]

This is confirmed by what immediately follows concerning the divergences among Marxists. It would seem at first glance that these divergences would inhibit anyone from saying anything about Marxism in the singular. However, the document continues with the affirmation of that fundamental unity, in spite of everything. Thus, taking a step that does not seem logical, after saying that Marxism "has become divided and has given birth to various currents which diverge significantly from one another," it adds: "To the extent that they remain *fully Marxist,* these currents continue to be based on certain fundamental tenets which are not compatible with the Christian conception of humanity and society" (VII,8). But if the Marxists are divided, who can decide what is *fully Marxist?*

It would be easy to dissipate that appearance of illogic by appealing to what we might call sociological statistics, i.e., the general

average: something that must commonly be seen by those who call
themselves Marxist, or those who attack them, or even those who
make statistics about them. That would be what the document calls
the common "fundamental tenets," adherence to which determines
why certain thinkers, and not others, are "fully" Marxist. But this
criterion has other serious drawbacks, and it does not seem to be
what grounds the reason (or even the need) for that singular Marxism
with its plurality of currents. In fact, what the document is interested
in detecting are, so to speak, "involuntary" Marxists. It is not interested in determining who, among Latin American theologians, *de-
clares himself to be* Marxist but rather who, even without saying so
or perhaps without wanting to be Marxist, nevertheless *is* one.

For that reason, it is necessary that there be a single "reality"
upon which all authentic Marxists would have to agree. It is enough,
according to the document, to practice certain analyses or to use
certain analytical elements for this method of knowing reality to
become a "determining principle" (VIII,1) that links its user, even
unintentionally, to the "ideological nucleus" proper to Marxism.
"Thus no separation of the parts . . . is possible. If one tries to
take only one part, say, the analysis, one ends up having to accept
the entire ideology" (VII,6).[5]

Later we will examine this character of an inevitable trap that
Marxism, and only Marxism, seems to possess. What interests us
here is to point out a previous difficulty. If determining that "fully
Marxist" has nothing to do with statistics (and only in this case could
one speak of a necessary unity among its elements) and does have
something to do with an inexorable *internal* logic, then what authority does the Church or its magisterium have to determine and declare
what Marxism *truly* is?

Without going into complicated theological considerations, it is
commonly accepted that the proper field of the ecclesiastical magisterium is the affirmations (and only affirmations) regarding faith.
Its clearest and most specific function consists in determining if such
statements do or do not conform to the traditional content of faith
that stems from the biblical revelation of God. In other words, the
magisterium judges the orthodoxy or heterodoxy of the expressions
that attempt to expound the Christian faith.

This function would be practically useless and even theoretically impossible if language did not have certain rules that anchored it, in a way, in a reality wider than the individual fact expressed. To say, for example, that "God does not exist" could not be judged from the point of view of orthodoxy if the term "God" could mean *any*thing. The magisterium works with the dictionary, in the sense that it attends to ordinary language. When that language is not clear, two paths are open. The magisterium can choose and explain the termi-, nology it is going to use and, with it, judge the statement in question, leaving the one who made it free to decide if that is what he or she wanted to say. Or it can go further and, from other statements by the same person (and in the same context) infer the meaning given to the word and, according to that meaning, finally judge the statement.

Note that in the latter case, the magisterium does not define the orthodoxy of the language but rather of the "thing" expressed. But it is still more important to point out that this internal logic, applied to the author of a statement, cannot serve to condemn him or her *before* he or she has made a properly theological statement. In the celebrated case of Galileo, the ordinary and fallible magisterium of the Church erred in believing that the inerrancy of the Bible supposed the material exactitude that Joshua had stopped the sun in its orbit to allow the Jews to pursue their enemies. But it erred further by condemning the theory that the earth revolved around the sun because the *logical consequence* would be that Joshua could not have stopped the sun's course. In the same vein, to say "I am a materialist" might even be considered a stupidity, but it is not a *theological* error. It is not a theological error until one comes to the seemingly inevitable conclusion that God does not exist.

This is not meant to claim that the function of the magisterium is so limited that it cannot warn of the danger of admitting things that "are seen not to be compatible with the Christian faith"—that is, that *logically* would lead to denying it.[6] There is the need, however, to carefully establish what properly or strictly belongs to the function of the magisterium: to define the orthodoxy or heterodoxy of the expressed thought, and to distinguish it from what only *prepares* for that function by warning of dangers, whether they come from the use of mistaken language or whether (and with greater reason) they come from admitting premises that logically would lead to deforming or negating the faith.

And since the *Instruction* affirms precisely this latter of Marxism (VI,9-10), we must suppose that whoever uses so-called "Marxist analysis" either has already reached (disguised in the language of a theology) the loss of the Christian faith or would have to arrive at that loss (as a logical consequence). Everything seems to indicate that the second part of the document discusses this last hypothesis, but it is a shame that it did not say so expressly and clearly.

Even so, it is hard to think that where there are as many opinions as there are heads—and that is what is true in Marxism today—we may still be facing a logic so strong that when one postulates any single element of analysis, the acceptance of the whole rest of the system must univocally and unequivocably follow. If this monolith exists, then, about what do the Marxists argue, and in what do they "diverge significantly"?

The dilemma is all the more difficult to avoid when the liberation theologians (at least as far as I know them, and even considering what the document says of them) take only *elements* (the famous "borrowing") of that analysis. What is more, as far as I know, they complement and correct those elements with analytical elements from other sources. If they were impossible to separate from the rest of Marxist thought, how is it that well-known non-Marxist and even anti-Marxist thinkers and sociologists—such as Weber or Mannheim—can use those analytical tools without being pushed to the same consequences? The Supreme Pontiff himself makes excellent use of Marxist analysis, such as the category of *alienation,* to describe the worker who gives up the fruits of his or her labor in exchange for a salary in capitalist (or socialist) systems.

Thus I believe that on the whole we must conclude that the document is fundamentally a *warning,* worthy of being noticed, about the danger that exists in the uncritical use of any method of analysis. Reality never dictates what method is to be used to analyze it. And there is no method that does not emphasize certain aspects of reality, favoring them over others (such as the analysis of Latin America's economic situation, a situation that has resulted in the death of millions of people by hunger and malnutrition). Therefore Latin Americans, perhaps more than others, do not have the luxury of being single-minded and simple-minded in our analysis of reality. We fully agree, of course, that every analysis, in order not to fall into the trap of reducing the explanation of reality to a single mechanism, must make a "careful epistemological critique" (VII,4).

There remains only to ask why the need was particularly felt to call attention to liberation theology. In effect, other theologies would be facing the same problem given that the limitation pointed out as the source of the danger "derives from the nature of human science" (VII,13). And to escape this danger, it is not enough to refuse to analyze reality.

Does Marxism—or better, do all Marxisms—have a distinct epistemological status that makes impossible what is possible (and in certain cases, easy) in other methods of analysis: to accept certain valid elements in order to understand the mechanisms of social processes, separating them from the rest of the system that perhaps integrates them into an ideology, a global view of the universe? The latter occurs, for example, with functionalism, but it would seem at first glance that using its elements would not imply the acceptance of a pragmatist philosophy that would relativize the very existence of God in its final metaphysical consequences. And if this were so, why are functionalism and Marxism not equally condemned?

Here we have, and I believe the reader will perceive it clearly, a *second* point—without having abandoned the first.

The strength with which the document denounces every use of Marxist analysis tells us that this is no mere general warning, but an act of the magisterium that points to something *logically* tied to the practical negation of faith: "We are facing, therefore, a real system, even if *some hesitate to follow the logic to its conclusion.* As such, this system is a perversion of the Christian message as God entrusted it to His church. *This message in its entirety finds itself then called into question by the 'theologies of liberation'"* (IX,1).

Following this, it is supposed that, in spite of the explosion of Marxism into different currents which "diverge significantly," to use the analytical tools of any of these currents (if they are "fully" Marxist) and to try to do Christian theology, is due to a lack of logic—similar to that of the self-proclaimed materialist who has not perceived or does not want to perceive that it means not believing in the existence of God.

Will the document leave us in the dark about the equivocal term "fully Marxist"? The answer is no, although one would have expected a more dispassionate and serious study of so central a term.

There is a key text, although very brief and somewhat strange, on what the document considers the "core" of Marxism. It says: "*Let us recall* the fact that *atheism and the denial of the human person, his liberty and his rights,* are at the *core* of the Marxist theory. This theory, then, contains errors which directly threaten the truths of the faith regarding the eternal destiny of individual persons. Moreover, to attempt to integrate into theology an analysis whose criterion of interpretation depends on this atheistic conception is to involve oneself in terrible *contradictions*" (VII,9). As is clear, this is not a condemnation but a serious warning of the magisterium that to admit certain things outside the theological plane would lead, if thought out logically and acted upon as such, to the denial of faith.

I said that this paragraph is strange: the first strangeness arises from the elements that are presented as the "core" of Marxism as well as the determinants of the way in which Marxism analyzes reality. It must not be forgotten that it is not enough that the "core" be contradictory to the faith; for the theological argument as presented here, it is necessary that the analysis must be done while admitting such core elements. Therefore, from that point of view, what one would least expect to find in the paragraph is an allusion to *atheism*. Certainly, no one ignores or doubts that Marx was an atheist, nor that almost all (if not all) the governments that fall under the label "Marxist" may (although to different degrees) develop an official atheistic propaganda. But I believe that no two Marxist thinkers would agree on in what sense and to what degree atheism constitutes a central element of Marxism.[7]

The divergences are very serious on this point, and the worst thing is that every position can quote Marx in its favor. For some, the tie between Marxism and atheism would be a kind of metaphysics, sometimes called dialectical materialism, even though Marx never used such a term. For others, Marxism has no metaphysics at all, and if it is atheistic, it is because of the relativization of every more or less abstract idea, a relativization that is produced by perceiving the dependence of such ideas on the economic context where the individual works and relates most closely with his or her peers—all of which would be equal to saying that so-called "historical materialism" would be the (indirect) cause of atheism. And for still others, Marx was an atheist simply because in his day so were the majority of radical thinkers or because the religion he knew seemed to support the status quo—which is the same as saying that, despite appearances, atheism is "accidental" in Marxism. Many others might say that to link Marxism and atheism would be nothing less than to deny one of the central points of Marxism—that it is a science and that the question of the existence of God does not enter into it.

Finally, there are those who may say (and not without reason when one looks at the content of atheistic propaganda in Marxist countries) that religion is fought not in the name of Marxism but in the name of a scientific world-view in general. In a word, the vast majority of Marxists who can *give reasons for their atheism* and who use logic most seriously do not consider atheism to be a core element of their thought. Will the Church be able to teach them what they should believe in order to be fully Marxist? Or will it ignore them and embrace what the "man in the street" (above all in the West) thinks about the relationship between Marxism and atheism?

Personally, I do not believe that it is even possible to pass over all these divergences and affirm that it is *impossible* to use elements of Marxist analysis without being led logically to accept that supposedly core element of the ideology: its atheism.

But it is even stranger that instead of a profound study of this question, so important for faith, and in a document where in order to *teach* it is necessary to get to the bottom of things, it only says "Let us recall that . . . ," as if this were a primer in the social sciences or in the history of philosophy for which it would be necessary only to pause briefly on this topic.

However, this brevity makes it much more difficult to "recall" that nothing less than the "denial of the human person, his liberty and his rights" is also at the core of Marxist theory. No one with even a little historical education can ignore the fact that Marxism (good or bad, right or wrong) was born precisely for the purpose of struggling against that denial. After speaking of the divergences that separate Marxists on the previous point (atheism), one should speak of the unanimous convergence of those who hold (as central to the system) the denial of that denial—the affirmation of people as members of a society which destroys their alienation and returns to them their liberty and rights.

To state that Marxism has not achieved this goal is one thing (and one would have to be careful to analyze whether it has not done so to any extent). To say it tries to do the opposite is something else altogether. I detect in the *Instruction* a note of hatred or, at least, of resentment. I can sympathize with this resentment because I suppose that behind it there is true suffering. But I believe that the magisterium of the Church cannot gain the respect it deserves when it loses its composure in so blatant a fashion.

Obviously, the defective results that accompany known socialist societies cannot be attributed solely—or with a simple "let us recall" —to "Marxist theory," and even less to its "core." That would be as unjust as to accept as the core and intention of Christianity the methods of the Inquisition or the style of life that has existed for centuries and continues to exist in Christian countries such as those of Latin America.

What is more, and I believe that this is at the heart of what the document tries to do: rightly, one should be able to discuss with Marxists, in good faith, whether such defects constitute accidental deviations or whether they are in some way linked to internal faults of the ideology or system, and then suggest what modification might correct them. That this is in the logic of the document—while the caricature is in its redaction—is demonstrated by the paragraph that follows: "This misunderstanding of the spiritual nature of the person leads to a total subordination of the person to the collectivity, and thus to the denial of the principles of a social and political life which is in keeping with human dignity" (VII,9). The statement seems clear in itself; however, in reality it is not, because those principles are similarly denied with equal intensity in "officially" Christian countries, where the spiritual nature of the person is considered dogma. If it were clear, it would not explain why, for example, in Latin America (since the document mentions that continent) the Christian *pathos* toward the misunderstanding of human dignity would lead to "taking refuge" (as the document indicates) in the very system that produces that denial, not only in reality but in principle.

Thus, we are not dealing so much with a "recall" as with a logical process which, while unperceived by many Marxists, is worthy of strict attention.

One of the ways to unravel this knotted skein is to destroy one of the common points that so negatively influences both sides of the issue: the use of the term "materialism." It is not as if Marx did not write about the spiritual needs of the human person. What he stated about the human relationships that work produces and about liberty and the vocational nature that one must have, so that the individual is fully realized and does not need to buy extra time for his or her spiritual and human development, is so similar to a personalist and Christian view of labor that John Paul II could take it up again, without danger of materialism or atheism, in his encyclical *Laborem Exercens*.

This does not prevent the terms "materialism" or "materialist" from perhaps playing a mistaken role, as much in Marx himself as in those who follow him. These terms deserve serious study by both sides, study in which the magisterium could have a clarifying role.

On the one hand, it can be argued that the continual use of the words "material," "materialism," and "materialist" is enough to force the conclusion that this conception of the human person excludes the *spiritual* aspect. Many Marxists will deny that and will even show that those terms play the same role in the system that "realism" plays in Western philosophy as being the opposite of "idealism" incarnated in Hegel, his predecessors, and his successors.[8] Add to this that Marx rejected both the materialist (mechanist) philosophers of his day and any philosophical *explanation* of reality, even if it were materialist, and concentrated instead on *changing* that reality.

But, on the other hand, one must ask to what point did Marx's radical mistrust of all "idealism" lead him (in his search for a change in social reality) to seek solid, unambiguous, undistorted, scientific, and finally, material means to find that new "non-materialist" person. The great lever that he envisioned for the transformation of society was the passing of ownership of the means of production from the individual to the collective. Is this to trust overly in some *thing* (material) that would be capable by itself to carry out a sufficient transformation so as to restore necessary dignity to the complexity of human existence?

Did this prepare the path that would lead his successors (without the same gifts) to the simplistic solutions of imposed plans, material reward and punishment, repression, and scorn or suspicion toward rich and complex religious traditions? It is true that many Marxists have noted this and have openly stated it. It would be a caricature to pretend that all Marxist currents are blind to this lacuna, just as it would be a caricature to think that it is enough to defend the "spirituality" of the human person to achieve a society where human rights are not violated.

While this brief discussion is not even the outline of a study, the one thing it shows is that as one purports to warn Christians of the dangers of accepting uncritically any element of Marxism, it is necessary to take upon oneself the task of showing what, for the authors of the document, is the Marxist system to which they refer and why they choose it among other possible interpretations. Once having done this, they should proceed to the epistemological examination that allows them to know what things are logically linked among themselves and what things can be used without leading to the logical obligation to accept the rest.

It is paradoxical that liberation theologians have done this work of defining what elements of Marxism to use and what to reject, while the document that accuses them of not having done so (see

VII,4) makes no such definition. Nor does the document seem even to recognize this fact.

Third, I believe the document does contain an explanation. Good or bad, it is an explanation, and to a certain point it is based on epistemological considerations. Although it may be just another "let us recall," it is certain that the document speaks in some way of the epistemological status of Marxism, even if it is not defined as such.

It has been said over and over again of Hegel's thought that whoever takes a step into his system never finds a way out of it. A parallel statement is made in the document: "The thought of Marx is such a global vision of reality that all data received from observation and analysis are brought together in a philosophical and ideological structure, which predetermines the significance and importance to be attached to them. The ideological principles come prior to the study of the social reality and are presupposed in it. Thus, no separation of the parts of this epistemologically unique complex is possible. If one tries to take only a part, say, the analysis, one ends up having to accept the entire ideology" (VII,6).

Who makes, or in the name of whom is made, this cardinal statement? It does not seem proper to theology to determine if this "epistemologically unique" character does or does not belong to Marxism, even if the document were able to tell us which is the "true" Marxism among its variations. It is a fact, however, that in a later paragraph it would seem that the ability to discern that character is attributed to theology, because the document states, "The ultimate and decisive criterion for truth can only be a criterion which is itself theological" (VII,10). But it is evident that this statement cannot be separated from its context, because it would mean that theology has the last word in any class of knowledge, from mathematics to sociology. The context indicates that the last word regarding "the *use of philosophical positions or of human sciences*" must be the object of a *theological* discernment.

It is not a case, then, of discerning whether it is possible to separate elements out of this complexity known as Marxism. It continues to be, as the document clearly and explicitly states, the object of a "careful epistemological critique" (VII,4), in which, obviously, theology does not have the last word. The certitude about the "unique" coherence of all the elements of Marxism will have to be studied. Only then, and in view of the results of that study, will theology be able to say if it is licit to use certain elements of analysis proper to the system in question, and to what extent—nothing more.

This brings us back once again to the point of departure, because this study is not done in the document. The magisterium takes as its task an affirmation—well understood as it is expressed here—that does not stem from a common logical ground. The myth of an impenetrable Marxism—or, worse still, easily penetrable but with doors closed to the outside—is, I believe, inspired by a anti-Marxist *pathos* (understandable as it may be among persons or groups who have had to suffer because of it). Such a myth cannot be accepted as a rigorously argued epistemological conclusion. One must add that, consciously or unconsciously, such *pathos* is intensified as the political power of Marxism in the world grows. It is therefore difficult to determine what is political and what is epistemological in the conception of Marxism held by the document.

Therefore, I believe the quote from *Octogesima Adveniens* of Paul VI in the document has more of a strictly epistemological value. It is a "warning" and "remains fully valid today": "it would be 'illusory and dangerous . . . to accept elements of the Marxist analysis without recognizing its connections with the ideology, or to enter into the practice of class-struggle and of its Marxist interpretation while failing to see the kind of totalitarian society to which this process slowly leads'" (VII,7; *Octogesima Adveniens,* 34).

The reader will have noted that the "intimate bond" of "connections" between analysis and ideology does not appear in Paul VI; he says, rather, that it is dangerous to fail to distinguish them. Every analysis that is dependent upon an ideological or philosophical system carries with it the risk of unconsciously and uncritically embracing theoretical presuppositions. But risk does not mean the logical necessity of falling into error, from which the theologian can be preserved only by his or her own lack of coherence or attention.

Conversely, in the quote from Paul VI, there is an element that is much more similar to an epistemological aspect that was highlighted some time before by John XXIII in *Pacem in Terris,* 159. In effect, the danger mentioned by the document is that of taking the *logical* step and falling into *theological* error. Not only in the first part but also in the second part of the document, the theology of liberation is accused of making an analysis, through class struggle, that logically would suppose a "historical immanentism"—which is the same as saying it would reduce the Gospel of salvation to an earthly gospel (see IX, 3-4).

Paul VI, on the contrary, points to a practical criterion that is an open door to that "epistemologically unique complex" which is Marxism according to the document: the danger is recognized *in history*. In effect, one does not cease denying God, or the truth, or transcendence, or orthodoxy. One ends by enslaving the individual. And for the one who began that struggle for the liberation of his or her brothers and sisters, there immediately arises critical reflection. We know, furthermore, that in that critique, Marxists in good faith intervene and raise doubts about elements in their own system.

This is more in line with the teaching of John XXIII, who did not speak of "epistemologically unique complexes" closed to all entrance, but rather of making

> a clear distinction between false philosophical teachings regarding the nature, origin, and destiny of the universe and of man, and movements which have a direct bearing either on economic and social questions, or cultural matters or on the organization of the state, even if these movements owe their origin and inspiration to these false tenets. While the teaching once it has been clearly set forth is no longer subject to change, the movements, precisely because they take place in the midst of changing conditions, are readily susceptible of change. Besides, who can deny that these movements, in so far as they conform to the dictates of right reason and are interpreters of the lawful aspirations of the human person, contain elements that are *positive and deserving of approval? (159)*.

*   *   *

What then are we to conclude? I believe I have demonstrated that the first part of the document presented, clearly and coherently, a

theology; and in all logic, that theology came down against liberation theology. The alleged reduction of the Gospel of salvation to the
immanent in history did not arise from the fact that "such and such"
an analysis of reality had been done. That conclusion would have
been arrived at with or without the use of the social sciences, with or
without class struggle, and with or without the use of violent means.
It was on the basis of a theological position, of a way of interpreting
the Word of God, that the document opposed liberation theology.

Moreover, convinced or not, if the reader has followed my argument in the first part, he or she will have perceived that for me the
issue discussed was broader than just liberation theology. On many
important points, what was being considered was *an entire period* of
the history of theology—the post-conciliar period.

But apparently that was not enough for the *Instruction*. One
could almost say that the document ignored everything it had said
before and, beginning with Chapter VII, searched for a new basis for
criticizing liberation theology. This could be summarized in a single,
two-sided factor—the use of Marxist analysis, and its theoretical
and practical consequences in theology.

But new problems arose here. For instance, to what degree did
that analysis continue to be "Marxist" when it was employed
outside the global ideological or philosophical system? Another
example: what was, down deep, *the* Marxism from which so many
distinct and divergent versions could be and were taken? And,
finally, is there a socially scientific uniqueness that makes it impossible to utilize one of its analytical tools without embracing the entire
system?

Although at first glance it seemed strange, I did not find any
logical response to any of these three questions. I did find statements
or certain common grounds without a corresponding investigation.
According to these statements, those elements continue to be tied to
the Marxist system. When these elements were thought to have been
separated from the system, Marxism recovered them—leading to
the denial of God and of the human person. This is because, epistemologically speaking, Marxism (according to the document) is a
singular case, one in which everything is so intrinsically united and

inseparable that it is impossible to use any one of its elements in isolation.

Even so, I understand that the magisterium here fulfills its function of warning against the *danger* of dogmatic and practical error. Not being on proper theological ground, it had to conform to the dictates of common sense so as not to enter into a quagmire of interpretations. This is enough to justify the serious warning, even though its basis is, as was expected, very much tied to prejudices and common feelings related to a period of tensions, threats, and cold wars on the political plane—a plane that anyone can see is present throughout the document, especially in its second part.

In such conditions, I do not see how a theological judgment on the use of Marxism can go much further than warn against dangers that are perceived only by superficial observation. We are not, as in the first part of the document, facing one theology judged by another. But this *minor* theological qualification I am giving to the second part might hide what may be the most salvageable and profitable aspect of the document. In pointing to areas much more precise than an entire theology, it invites liberation theology to reflect on various specific issues.

If it is admitted, as I hope it is, that the theology of liberation does not deserve the condemnation given it in the first part, the second part may be very useful. And this is precisely the program for the critical reading that will have to be done of Chapters VIII-XI— because VII is the one that has allowed us to attempt what is usually called a *theological qualification*.

From Class Struggle to Violence

I believe it necessary to begin this critical reading with the Marxist analysis of historical reality and of the place that *class struggle* holds in it as its "fundamental structure" (VIII,5; see IX,2 as well). From this "structure" it will be deduced that not only is society "founded on violence" (VIII,6) but that violence is the only way to overthrow the present situation—the oppression of some social classes by others. In turn, according to the *Instruction*, this will lead to establishing an ethic where "it is the transcendent character of the distinction between good and evil, the principle of morality, which is implicitly denied" (VIII,9). Finally—in the last link of this logical chain—we find the inversion of the right relationship between immanence and transcendence with regard to God himself and his word: "every affirmation of faith or of theology is subordinated to a political criterion, which in turn depends on the class struggle, the driving force of history" (IX,6). This appears very much like atheism, or at least a denial of the transcendental character that must be given to the theoretical and practical truth about God, his salvation, his Church, and his sacraments (see IX,1-2,8,13).

Before attempting to say no to all, let us review the links in the chain one by one.

1. There is the question of class struggle as the instrumentality, central and inseparable in Marxist analysis. Several points need to be made here.

First of all, the concept of class struggle is applied, strictly speaking, to modern society. And it would not be very accurate to make class struggle, solely and in every age, the "driving force of history." What Marxism—which did not invent such conflict—maintains is that, when labor is diversified and the primitive horde gives way to supposedly complementary types of differentiated labor, these types are in fact distributed unequally among the members of the society in question. First, certain individuals, then certain groups, and later certain social classes take control of certain types of easier, more pleasant, more profitable, more prestigious, and more significant types of work. The others must carry out the more difficult tasks, and when hiring workers for salary enters upon the social scene, these others receive more modest remuneration.

The second point is that this is not an extremely original invention. Several Fathers of the Church had already denounced the fact that when there were rich and poor in a society, it was due neither to nature nor to God but rather to the progressive appropriation, by the rich, of goods that the Creator had destined for the common good.[9]

One could almost say that social analysis based on the suspicion that structural differences are due to the wrongful appropriation of common goods is more Christian than Marxist. The explanation why this theological fact has been forgotten is that, during the kind of *Christian order* that was the rule during the Middle Ages, there was, first, a certain measure of leveling, in practice, of the more obvious inequalities and, second, of theoretically justifying by Christian doctrine itself (as mere *administration*), what was not possible or desirable to level. That justification, to the point of attributing to the will of God the existence of unequal social *classes,*[10] has come to be (although it is later implicitly contradicted by the magisterium) part of the social doctrine of the Church. It is thus understandable that elements of the purest Christian tradition are suspected of being borrowed from Marxism.

Two things, one positive and one negative, should be recognized in this first stage of analysis. The positive aspect is that the world in general has been living in a context of *scarcity,* from which arises the dramatic, unjust, and in many cases scandalous appropriation of common goods. Moreover, every individual, group, or class defended its privileged place in the division of labor, *institutionalizing* what was first obtained by force or cunning. This justification or legalization of privileges obtained in a world of scarcity forms a very important part of the juridical, social, cultural, and political mechanisms or structures of every existing society, even those that are—to some degree—islands of abundance in a terribly suffering world.

As was noted previously, the more needy that world is, the more difficult it is for a society to integrate efficiently and capably all of its members. Some will be better integrated; their vocations will be more respected, their opinions better heard, their work schedules easier. Others will be marginalized in one way or another in the sense that only on rare occasions will their opinions be asked. Their personal vocation will not be taken into account but only their quantitative contribution to the work force, and (in practice) an exhausting manual activity will be asked in exchange for what is needed to survive or, even less, so that they may survive as best they can without disturbing the established social order.

These are facts recognized by the document (see VII,12, etc.), and no Marxist is needed either for them to exist or, at least in general, for them to be considered. Moreover (and this is most important), anti-Marxist authors and books may be cited that use this analysis—of the social structures of inequality and the struggle of unequally endowed classes—against political Marxism. They study, in that context of conflict, what means can be used so that a society described in such an artificial and inhuman way does not succumb to its own institutionalized inequality.

The negative aspect of this analysis is its one-sidedness, either real or potential. Although it may be logical to think, as St. Ambrose says, that "avarice determines the rights of ownership," not every dehumanizing division of labor seems to stem from exacerbated economic interest, or at least it does not disappear with economic equality. Many other inequalities—racial, sexual, religious, and so on—have come to be connected with economic inequalities, converging with them to produce social marginalization. This is a point at which Marxist analysis is often shown to be blind or simplistic. However, many Marxists, above all cultural anthropologists and sociologists, have denounced it.

The need not to treat injustice as simply individual cases is a constant doctrine of the magisterium of the Church, especially in recent times. This implies "the authentic, if obscure, perception of the dignity of the human person, created 'in the image and likeness of God' (Gen 1:26-27), ridiculed and scorned in the midst of a variety of different oppressions: cultural, political, racial, social and economic, often in conjunction with one another" (1,2).

Medellín is distinguished, furthermore, because therein the magisterium of the Church shows Christians that they can be sinning—although strictly speaking they may be doing nothing—in a structurally unjust and violent society. In effect, the structures themselves reproduce violence, injustice, and dehumanization without anyone's *direct* intervention, but with everyone's complicity.

2. But social analysis does not end here. On the contrary, it only begins. In effect, the vast majority of Marxists will agree that the analysis of social reality, pointing out conflict or class struggle, not only brings to light an explanation of how society functions but provides a means to transform it. But, again, this is not a Marxist discovery, and therefore it should not be used to label as more or less Marxist those who use it. It is common sense to see that the moments

of greatest activity and creativity (both in individual and collective history) are those of crisis, and not those of calm.

Capitalism itself uses a similar concept according to which competition is a conflict between opposed interests; necessary social changes will be made precisely not by stopping competition through an external arbiter, but by unshackling it. To suppress competition, according to capitalism, is to suppress conflict at the risk of introducing paralysis. Capitalism presupposes that conflict liberates and purifies human aggression and channels it toward work, invention, and creation. Finally, it was Hegel and not Marx who presented the progress of humanity in self-awareness as the fruit of conflicts. Marx was not the inventor of the dialectic of slave and master as the principle of civilization.

But perhaps the document is right in passing over this subject of exact genealogies. Its emphasis is that "it is not the *fact* of social stratification with all its inequity and injustice, but the *theory* of class struggle as the fundamental law of history which has been accepted by these 'theologies of liberation' as a principle" (IX,2; original italics). And they take this principle not from Hegel but from Marx. That is why the Vatican document simply attributes to Marxism the idea that class struggle is "the fundamental structure of history" (VIII,5) or, if one prefers, its "driving force" (IX,3 and 6).

It would be interesting to ask what would be the conclusion if it were supposed that "class struggle" and the *search for justice* were synonymous. The document itself, speaking of the *fact* of those conflicts, points to "injustice" that is added to mere social inequality (IX,3). Those marginalized by society seek to be integrated into it (aided by all those who, although from other classes, embrace the same value of justice); this leads to the successive conflicts that threaten those who do not want their privileges reduced. In this way, the search for justice in society would be "the driving force of history."

Nevertheless, there are two reasons, intimately linked, why the document cannot accept that conclusion. The first consists in another parallel that is subtly introduced: conflict is synonymous with violence; whoever says violence does not say justice. The second reason consists in an interpretation (perhaps doubtful and not very logical but certainly common) of what "class struggle" means in practice if it must be the fundamental structure or driving force of history: to identify the "class enemy" and as such act against it.

In a word, it would seem that class struggle cannot be the driving force of history for an *objective* reason: class struggle as the mainspring of history would mean that society is constructed upon violence; and for a *subjective* reason: class struggle divides people, making them recognize each other as friends or enemies, worthy of love or hate, according to the social class to which they belong.

I believe that one of the most important elements of the criticism of Marxist analysis and its use by liberation theologians begins to show itself here. Conflict is more than a repeated and general *fact* for Marxist analysis. Therefore, according to the document, 'it is not the fact . . . but the theory of class struggle as the *fundamental law* of history which has been accepted by these "theologies of liberation"'(IX,2). Now then, what does accepting this fundamental law imply? It "implies that society is founded on violence" (VIII,6).

At first glance, it is not easy to see the logical reason for this move from conflict to violence. Why does class struggle have to lead to violence if the former is understood to be the effort that every unequal and unjust society makes to better integrate all of its members, when the marginalized are awakened to the consciousness that they can and must achieve a better integration, even if this effort may collide with those who hold class privileges within that society? Moreover, why would the society in that case be *based* on violence? Can it be said simply, for example, that France or the United States is *based* on violence because their social structures stem historically from violent revolutions, out of which some of their principal social problems were solved? One must not forget that, starting from very similar situations and having to resolve the basic conflict of human rights of those who did not belong to the nobility, France and England arrived at democratic societies by different paths: one with a violent revolution and the other without one.

There are, however, Marxists who pretend that society is based on violence simply because class struggle may be the historical main-spring that drives societies to their deepest structural changes. Not seeing very much logic in that may explain the position of liberation theologians. Many will accept, because reality seems to manifest it, the so-called class struggle (or "conflict," so that "struggle" may not be understood as necessarily armed struggle) as an element of Marxist analysis, but no one I know accepts as a fact that society *must* therefore be based on violence.

However, it is possible that the next paragraph in the document may explain the logic that would allegedly lead Marxism to such a conclusion. It alludes to what I said previously—that the document presents Marxism as pretending that class struggle is an "objective, necessary law" and one which is grounded "scientifically" (VIII,7). This would appear to be an allusion to the Marxist conception of the dialectic, or at least to *one* Marxist conception of it—one that perhaps is more Hegelian than Marxist. But that is of little impor-tance for the moment. We are seeking where and how we are warned of a real danger that liberation theology must take notice of.

It is well known that many Marxists—led by Engels—deny that Marx had thought of a determinism, since this would be a denial of his attempt to change the world instead of merely *explaining it*. But neither is it possible to deny that Marx is ambiguous with respect to this; nor should it be overlooked that all of his work does not entail a strictly logical development.

There is, anyway, a simplistic, official Marxism—*ad usum Delphini*—in which the dialectic is reduced to a simple determinism that is valid for all conflicts and that can predict where and how they are going to surface in history. According to this deterministic and mechanical understanding of the dialectic, conflicts occur, grow, and expand in consciousness and virulence, and thus arrive at the inevitable point of *violence* where the progressive forces overturn the negation that injustice imposes upon them.

In some places in his work, at least, this was Marx's thought. Even without detailing the amount of violence that would be neces-sary for the final step, he proposed that the general impoverishment

of the English sub-proletariat would bring about, "with the inexora-
bility of a natural process" (*Das Kapital,* I, part VIII, ch. 32), a
revolution in English society and, with it, the negation of the negation in the system of ownership. In this way—and with greater
ingenuity, in view of an even greater historical experience and political complexity—many Marxists in Latin America believe that the
increase of oppression by military dictatorships foreshadows the
inexorable fall of the global political-economic system and the rise
of socialism.

This is how one could explain what may appear to be a law in
Marxism (again, which Marxism?) that history progresses through
syntheses created out of *violence.* In this sense, then, some might say
that violence is the basis of society.

However, reading Engels with regard to the dialectic (applied to
nature, of course, but a fortiori applied to history), one can see that
he does not think of it in this simplified and deterministic way, but
rather as the varied development of conflicts that might result in
violence but that also might be resolved before arriving at that point,
or that might be maintained indefinitely.

If this is the case, we are again facing the practical demonstration
of the fact that Marxism—far from being an epistemologically
unique, compact monolith in virtue of its internal logic—is an epistemologically hybrid amalgam. This is the same as saying that each
part not only can be but should be recognized as disparate; and this
is not difficult to do.

This does not distract from the fact that there may be the possibility of a theologian—accepting social conflict as the driving force
which leads society in search of justice—mistakenly concluding that
society *must* necessarily pass through violence. But in such a case,
one would have to say that this is not the result of Marxist logic but
of its simplistic deformation. Even so, there is some value in the
document's calling attention to that possibility. In any event, let it be
clear that, leaving aside this point about a violence that would be
basic, we are not abandoning the subject of the use of violence; we
will have to return to this shortly.

Nevertheless, my impression is that the document points to a
more serious danger—or, to be more exact, to a danger that it judges

to be more serious as being more directly related to the Christian message. The second reason why it is impossible to identify class struggle with the search for justice is that class struggle is expressed by a *subjective* attitude that is not Christian—a continual intention to destroy the enemy of the class. In effect, "entrance into the class struggle is presented as a requirement of charity itself. The desire to love everyone here and now, despite his class . . . is denounced as counterproductive and opposed to love" (IX,7).

The document makes a laudable effort to escape the stereotype that presents *hatred* as the attitude of the Marxist in class struggle. But it warns that this struggle logically signifies identifying the enemy and that "it is claimed nevertheless that, if he belongs to the objective class of the rich, he is *primarily* a class enemy to be fought" (IX,7; original italics). Thus, while this objective placement in the struggle does not vary, "the universality of love of neighbor" will be inhibited by class enmity and will be able to flourish only when that situation has changed.[11]

I recognize that this is one of the more intricate problems that the Gospel, from its very beginning, has had to face. If I am not mistaken, it does not, nor will it, have a clear and satisfactory solution but only approximations that will minimize the dangers and thus suggest how human beings (who are not able to undo their emotions) can collaborate with the kingdom of God already mysteriously present in history (*Gaudium et Spes,* 39).

The difficulty, certainly affecting liberation theology, has nothing to do with its method of analyzing reality. It arises from reality itself. It does not stem from whether or how class struggle is analyzed, but from the fact that it exists.

That is why the expression that the document uses sounds strange: "entrance into the class struggle." Where was the person before such a possibility presented itself? Whence does one enter into it? From a social peace? One can respond to this question only by reading the *data* that the document itself presents about that struggle. According to it, the only one who can enter into class struggle is one who is ignorant of its magnitude, its depth, or its consequences. The conflict already existed, and I believe that the whole world must agree that it is not Marxist analysis that introduced it. That analysis will be, at most, a means of better recognizing the enemy and the weapons the enemy holds.

This does not mean going *from* not having enemies to having them. Moreover, recognizing the conflict in its depth—and even the moral indignation in the face of this "ridiculed and scorned image of God," as the document says—is the only way of being able to end it. An illness is not cured without diagnosis. That is the price of peace, the magisterium of the Church at Medellín tells us, because "there always will be attempts against peace where unjust inequalities among men and nations prevail" (*Conclusions,* II:14).[12]

The Vatican document further recognizes the necessity of paying this price of opening the individual's consciousness to the full dimensions of the already-existing conflict. It does so when it says that "in revealing to them their vocation as children of God, *the Gospel has elicited* in the hearts of mankind a demand and a positive will for a peaceful and just fraternal life. . . . *Consequently,* mankind will no longer passively submit to crushing poverty. . . . It resents this misery as an *intolerable violation* of native dignity. Many factors, and among them certainly the *leaven of the Gospel,* have contributed to an *awakening of the consciousness of the oppressed*"(I,3-4).

This does not mean creating a false peace (see Jer 6:14) so that people may love each other despite injustices. Peace is the fruit of justice (*Gaudium et Spes,* 78) and not the reverse. But because this awakening of the consciousness of the oppressed is attributed, among other causes, to the "leaven of the Gospel" and because this esoteric designation can be ignored by some Christians, it is worth going to the Gospel.

In effect, the problem is presented to Jesus himself. In the same Q source where we find his teaching of love of one's enemies (Mt 5:44; Lk 6:27), we find Jesus' observation about the immediate result that his life and message will have: "Do not suppose that my mission on earth is to spread peace. My mission is to spread, not peace, but division. I have come to set a man at odds with his father, a daughter with her mother, a daughter-in-law with her mother-in-law: in short, to make a man's enemies those of his own household" (Mt 10:34-36; see also Lk 12:51-53).

Will one have to conclude that Jesus came to destroy the possibility of the very universal love he recommends? Or is it that this must be understood within that divisive context that will break the deepest ties between human beings and that will never disappear from Jesus' life nor that of his followers (cf. Mt 5:10-12; Lk 6:22-23)?[13] There can be no doubt that divisiveness is given in the text as the very reason for the gospel mission: "I have come to. . . ." No other external factor has brought it in, much less a particular method of analysis. It is the very message of Jesus coming into a historical context where a human society destroys the image of God in the person whom it marginalizes.

Because they seem to me totally pertinent, I quote and make my own (not knowing how better to express them) the words of Gustavo Gutiérrez "There are no situations, no matter how difficult they may be, that imply an exception or a parenthesis to the universal demands of Christian love."

I quote these words in trembling, not because I doubt their truth but because I am conscious of the difficulty of practicing them. And I will insist that the magisterium itself takes away any facile solution like the one of a pure neutrality in that conflict. Universal love continues to be my duty once I have opted for justice and for the poor who are deprived of it. The class enemy does not cease to be a human being whom we must love—and love effectively. But this does not mean he or she ceases to be a class enemy—just as those who rejected the good news of the kingdom of God did not cease to be the enemies of Jesus. There is no analysis that makes that opposition disappear and thus allow one to love more easily. How to love efficaciously in the midst of struggle and choice is and always will be a challenge to one's Christian creativity. Because one must opt; one must choose sides.

I continue, then, without understanding what kind of unusually strong logic should lead me from the analysis of social classes and their conflict—including the objective and subjective aspects—to relegating the practice of Christian love to eschatological reconciliation. I prefer to consider the "class struggle," of which Marxism speaks, as a search for justice—a search that, in the history of humanity and its sins, must be undertaken in a context of conflict.

That is the difficulty but also the richness and complexity of what must be my subjective Christian attitude.

I understand why the document must point out to Christians the risk of confronting that difficulty without a clear and solid Christian formation. Here, *as in any other instance of an option* (toward the left or the right), there will always be the temptation of over-simplification. There is no Marxist monopoly on this. I believe that the document itself, if one were to take it literally, would lead us to see in every Marxist an individual committed to the permanent negation of the human person and of his or her freedom and rights (see VII,9). I suppose that this is precisely what the document wants to avoid when the other person is analyzed as *nothing more than* a "class enemy," systematically seen as a monster without a soul, without exploring—for example, in a context of struggle—all the possibilities of "dialogue and persuasion" (IX,7).[14]

3. One thus arrives at a central problem, a problem that certainly goes beyond the limits of liberation theology and affects all post-Enlightenment thought—both secular and theological. It is the problem that links these three elements: *praxis*-option (in the sense of rationally or theoretically instituted practice), relativity, and (hermeneutical) interpretation.

I may have been unjust—and without a doubt I have seemed so—in what has preceded. The document seems to be filled with a resentment that leads to a caricature, and this discredits its critique, which otherwise should be recognized and listened to by the theology of liberation—because it needs it: not in order to be suppressed but in order to grow.[15]

I am not the first to see that not only liberation theology but the Marxism and social sciences of today, the various currents of psychoanalysis, the historical sciences (among them, the biblical ones), and even the modern physical-biological sciences, all carry the mark of an irreversible historical phenomenon: the Enlightenment—or as some say, the mark of the first and second Enlightenment.

The Enlightenment began optimistically the task of rationalizing those areas of human knowledge hitherto subjected to criteria that were considered nonrational; it assumed that reason was capable of raising clearer and more solid norms for thinking and therefore for action. But the result was quite different. It did not fail, but it was faced with a startling discovery. As it advanced, it realized that the truth avoided the most "scientific," simple, and immutable interpretations; it seemed to allow only the approach of the researcher, to immediately tell him or her that his or her search (even though sincere) was full of irrational elements that make every interpretation, every norm, and every calculation relative and provisory. The relativity in the physical world had its counterpart in the relativity of human judgments according to the social or psychological situation in which they were made. Not even the Word of God escaped those "pre-understandings." Even when truth was thought to be possessed, Christians were warned to "seek the truth" (*Gaudium et Spes,* 16).

The document we are studying here is particularly clear on this point and exposes the root of the problem. However, I believe it could have profited from a more global consideration, one less subject to its dominant preoccupation with Marxist analysis. Once, again, it is not because of the use of this analysis that theology (and not only liberation theology) must pose the hermeneutical issue.

Let me give an example. I have been able to observe what at times occurs in circles of psychologists and/or people involved in psychoanalysis (especially when they have a predominantly theoretical knowledge of it). Once I saw the effect produced by those circles on a person who, for some reason, joined the group from a different and, so to speak, "profane" situation (so as not to use the condemned word "normal"). That person led a life organized around principles whose foundation had never been questioned psychologically and which were no more or no less coherent than those of any other person. The impact that psychoanalysis insensitively produced in that individual stemmed from the repeated use of a method (not necessarily directed at that person) that suspects hermeneutically that the majority of the norms that guide human conduct constitute a patchwork of repressions.

Within such a group (and I am not criticizing the therapeutic *use* of psychoanalysis but only psychoanalysis as a universal explanation), at the end of a certain period of time, one concludes that it is impossible for one to be the exception that proves the rule and that the principles that were thought to have been accepted for their intrinsic value must be nothing other than the result of unconscious repressions. Although it may seem ridiculous, the need to show oneself as "uninhibited" or to destroy the supposed inhibitions ends, as in many cases I have personally known, by taking the place of the norms that were previously held. And this occurs without there appearing more pathological symptoms than those any other human being carries within.

Once more, this is a general phenomenon of the culture. Contrary to the previous criticism leveled by the document (in which it pointed to the analysis of reality without confronting that reality), here it touches upon the question of all modern hermeneutics linked to praxis. It does not mean only Marxist analysis as a consequence of the praxis of class struggle. The shame of being "bourgeois"—like the shame of being "inhibited," like the shame of being "fundamentalist" in the reading of the Bible and its norms, like the shame of being a "creationist" in the scientific study of biological evolution—all this constitutes a much more general phenomenon, which is always related to hermeneutics and the Enlightenment, and which must be treated as such.

This does not prevent the document from presenting here the problem as exclusively related to Marxist analysis. The presentation is intelligent and logical in its core, and I believe that liberation theology must confront it.

The first thing to note is that the *objective* situation within the class struggle conditions the *analysis* of that situation and also of *what happens* within it. The situation, in practice, is considered objective not so much because the subjectivity of the analyzer does not intervene but because the analysis (far from being able to avoid being partial) makes the situation its object. "The 'analysis' is inseparable from the *praxis,* and from the conception of history to which this *praxis* is linked. The analysis is for the Marxist an instrument of criticism, and criticism *is only one* stage in the revolutionary struggle" (VIII,2). It is superfluous to add that this revolution is the one that opts for the "proletariat."

I have added the emphasis to "is only one" for a reason that will be evident later and that even now the reader can foresee: it is not clear why the document goes from the indubitable fact to a dubious limitation. Logically, it would seem that it would be sufficient to say "it is *a* stage in the revolutionary struggle," adding (if one wants) "only those who engage in the struggle can work out the analysis correctly" (VIII,3).

Nevertheless, even taking the text as it is, one notes an important element. In spite of the belicose language, the "revolutionary struggle" of the proletariat does not make express mention of violent means. Moreover, we have already shown that if it is understood that class struggle means that society is founded on violence, the conclusion is not valid, nor does such logic (or lack of logic) have to be accepted by everyone who employs this kind of analysis.

On the other hand (and this is the value of the logic with which the document begins to treat the subject of praxis), the point that analysis is carried out from a particular place in the struggle is correct. One's opponent also does it that way, no matter what kind of analysis is used. The struggle is not analyzed out of nothing or from sheer "objectivity"—the latter kind of neutrality is epistemologically impossible.

That is what the magisterium of the Church in Medellín teaches us to do when it speaks to us of analyzing reality from the *option* for the poor. Only those who participate in that conflict with a praxis oriented by such an option can work out the analysis correctly. This is the "special concern for the poor and the victims of oppression, which in turn begets a commitment to justice" (III,3).

Undoubtedly, this logical consequence has been perceived by the document, and it tries to obviate it. The document says it is true that the "theologies of liberation" deserve "credit for restoring to a place of honor the great texts of the prophets and of the Gospel in defense of the poor," but those "theologies" lead to "a disastrous confusion between the *poor* of the Gospel and the *proletariat* of Marx" (IX,10). If the poor are the "victims of oppression," why would the "proletariat" not belong to this category? Only because Marx defended them and therefore, they may be called, very improperly, the "proletariat of Marx"?[16]

Even so, let us take one more step. The examination of an analysis of class struggle or (if what has been said is true) the examination of a praxis of the option for the poor and the oppressed will lead, according to the document, to the conclusion that "the only true consciousness, then, is the *partisan* consciousness." This means that "the concept of truth itself" is relativized. "It is totally subverted: there is no truth, they pretend, except in and through the partisan praxis" (VIII,4).

Remember, before making any value judgments, that "in the human and social sciences it is well to be aware above all of the plurality of methods and *viewpoints,* each of which reveals only *one aspect* of reality which is so complex that it defies simple and univocal explanations" (VII,5) and that highlighting "certain aspects of the reality while leaving others in the shade" is a limitation (recognized only after the Enlightenment) that *"derives from the nature of the human sciences"* (VII,13). From all this, one realizes it is difficult to find as a consequence that one is more universal, if one begins with a non-marxist analysis of reality. Or to put it in Christian terms: pretending that, instead of the option for the poor, "neutrality and indifference in the face of the tragic and pressing problems of human misery and injustice" (Introduction) assures people of transcending all partisanship.

In other words, the hermeneutical problem becomes even more difficult than it first seemed to be. Leaving aside for the moment that which can bring to its solution a revealed truth (that is, the "theological application of this core," the heading of chapter IX), the problem of the "ethical requirements" (VIII,7) that respect "the transcendent character of the distinction between good and evil, the principle of morality" (VIII,9) would seem to have no solution.

Another element, which must be taken into account to pose the problem correctly, is that things are exaggeratedly simplified when one speaks of a "partisan praxis." For example (in agreement with Medellín), is the option for the poor—within their conflict generated by the universal search for justice in a structurally unjust society—a "partisan" praxis? Yes, perhaps as a starting point. But the premise that guides the praxis—that "the fruit of justice is peace"—is already present at that starting point. The partisan option *for justice* thus appears as the intention to achieve, in reality and not merely "in the air," a greater universality: *peace.* The partiality of the former option is not destined to perpetuate itself as a limitation but rather as a way to overcome that limitation. Neither is it destined to be complemented—to be made more universal—by the opposite party, but rather it is intended to destroy the attempts of this party to paper over the conflict and to justify an already existing oppression, if we must believe in the document.

Does not the same thing happen when the conflict is analyzed in terms of class struggle and a partisan praxis is adopted within it? The document seems to say no. That praxis, according to the document, would have the following object: "to the violence which constitutes the relationship of the domination of the rich over the poor, there corresponds the counter-violence of the revolution, *by means of which this domination will be reversed*" (VIII,6). That is to say, the partisan praxis will be eternalized, passing from one adversary to its opposite—once the poor have obtained victory and reduced the rich to poverty.

The document *knows* that this is neither the function of class struggle nor of any analysis that studies the conditions of this struggle. And I say that the document knows this because it states so in another place: "the class struggle as a road toward a classless society is a myth" (XI,11). It cannot ignore this because Marxism, even in its most simplistic and official forms, repeats it endlessly. Why then not include this important fact at this point in the argument where it is truly important (if only with regard to the presumed intention of the adversary)? Without a doubt, the document did not judge it useful for the clarity or the strength of the argument that it is developing. But perhaps it does not understand that placing in one's opponent's mouth what one would like him or her to say detracts from serious argumentation.

It may or may not be true that achieving greater justice will bring a peace that transcends the partisan options that must previously be made. It may or may not be true that class struggle will lead, sooner or later, to a society without class conflict (which does not mean without problems). What is important is to analyze how, with what ethical principles, and with what norms this praxis is conducted. Only in this way (to return to the question at hand) will one be able to know if partisan praxis—linked to the option for the poor or to class struggle—endangers the transcendence of the distinction between good and evil: the principle of morality.

In fact, I believe this problematic relationship between partisan praxis and transcendent truth is not *specifically* related to Marxist analysis. The recognition of the conditioning that affects our knowledge of reality and our approximation of the truth is proper to all of today's social sciences.

Hence, one must be convinced that the problem is real, and whoever makes a "praxical" option for the poor must pose the question. Marxists themselves pose it; it is the least that Christians can do.

Partisan praxis in class conflict or struggle cannot, because of its option for justice, forget the problem that injustice uses violent means to impose itself. The document itself (not to mention Medellín) recalls this. It is not probable in such a case that justice—the justice from which peace is expected—would be achieved voluntarily. Therefore "the conception of truth," depending on a partisan praxis, goes "hand in hand with the affirmation of *necessary violence,* and so, of a *political amorality* (VIII,7) to a "violence" that is answered with the *"counter-violence* of the revolution" (VIII,6).

The issue is very well stated, and no one will be able to deny that it is a real problem. Even more so, one may note that the theology of liberation has not always questioned itself at this level. Notwithstanding, the question will be rightly posed as long as two elements (often commonly deformed) are remembered or perceived.

The first element in that problem is posed between the partisan analysis (class struggle) and political amoralism, as the document itself indicates. Violence and "revolution," in the strict sense, are seen as examples of areas where that amoralism would manifest itself.

There would be no objection to this if the ecclesiastical magisterium in Latin America had not posed the problem more correctly. And I use the term "more correctly" because examples of violence that might draw attention away from the clearer cases of political amoralism—and even real violence—may produce in the long run a "grave ambiguity in the heart of the readers" (to use an expression that the document applies in another case).

Medellín makes an analysis of the Latin American reality, using as a hermeneutic principle the option for the poor, which is obviously partisan. From that option, Medellín sees violence not as rising from revolution but from injustice: "The oppression by groups in power can give *the impression of maintaining peace* and order, but in truth it is nothing more than 'a permanent and unavoidable *seed of rebellion and war*' " (*Conclusions*, II:14. The final quotation is from Pope Paul VI).

Who is brought to mind by the words "necessary violence"? Medellín makes it very clear: "[The Christian] recognizes that in many respects Latin America is facing a situation of injustice that can be called *institutionalized violence.* . . . Therefore we should not be surprised that the 'temptation to violence' emerges in Latin America. One cannot try the patience of a people who have suffered for many years in a situation that is *unacceptable* for anyone with the least awareness of human rights" (*Conclusions*, II:16).

This leads one to believe that here it is not class analysis nor the partisan option which gives rise to "political amoralism." Otherwise, the position of the bishops would itself be called political amoralism. However, those who have made another partisan option in the class struggle will certainly not fail to call it so.

It is true that the Medellín document is somewhat ambiguous. It emphasizes violence that is cloaked in peace and order (and is thus presented to the whole world through the media) to safeguard unjust institutions. It says that those institutions are a seed of violence and that one cannot try the patience of the people by crushing in an intolerable way their human rights. But *it does not say what to do in such cases*. Medellín states that violence will result. It leaves blank who must or will take responsibility for what (according to the preceding) would seem to be expected or feared to happen: counter-violence (as the Vatican document here calls it).

This is very serious, because Christians cannot be mere spectators. Will one have to urge an absolute patience because violence is a "temptation"? What role does the Church play in view of the victims of institutionalized violence? I believe that this vacillation, which is badly concealed by rhetoric, demonstrates what I have been asserting: after the Enlightenment, it is more difficult to interpret reality and the norms for acting within it. What is relative, what is conditioned in our judgments, has been made more apparent in all areas, including that of violence.

However, it will be said, does the Christian not have clear norms by which to judge Latin America with regard to violence? This is where the second common ground comes into play. Summarily, this is the one that makes the problem of violence a "typically" Latin American (theological) problem, a problem that rises like a ghost as soon as one hears of liberation theology. But violence?

It is necessary, then, to unveil this unknown before proceeding with the study of the possible relationship between the analysis of class struggle and political amoralism.

Medellín holds two criteria about violence which must be taken as complementary, although the first one refers to a general principle and the second to what is considered an exception. The two stem from the same supreme magisterial authority, Pope Paul VI.

The first of these two criteria is that "violence is not Christian or evangelical. . . . Violence, or 'armed revolution' generally 'provokes new injustices, introduces new inequalities, and causes new disasters; one cannot fight a real evil when the price is a greater evil.' " Keeping in mind that the primary violence is the institutionalized one, the bishops at Medellín continue: "With Paul VI, we understand that this attitude [of those who react with counter-violence] often finds its ultimate motivation in noble aims of justice and solidarity" (*Conclusions*, II:19).

Medellín thus arrives at the second criterion valid for Christians, and does so by again quoting Paul VI: "It is true that revolutionary insurrection can be legitimized in the case of a manifest and prolonged 'tyranny that attacks the fundamental rights of the person and places in danger the common good of the nation' which proceeds from persons or structures that are clearly unjust" (ibid.).[17]

Liberation theology does not have or use any other principles than those that have just been mentioned and whose source, as can be seen, is not particularly Latin American. The one who proposes these principles is the Supreme Pontiff himself; nor are we talking about a perilous application of a remote principle to an unexplored and misunderstood reality. Although it could have been done, it would be difficult to qualify so nuanced a judgment as political amoralism.[18]

Nevertheless, this does not resolve our problem, although it does focus it better. What has happened so that (overnight and symptomatically with regard to Latin America) what has been until now the traditional doctrine of moral theology concerning the just war has been abandoned and is now viewed in terms of the danger of political amoralism? In my view, it is clear that the two possible sources for fixing clearly applicable norms in this area have suffered the erosion of the Enlightenment.

One was the *biblical* source. When it is stated that "violence is neither Christian nor evangelical," a fact is enunciated. But if one wants to draw from this a norm that is valid for any circumstance, one would have to complete the sentence and say that violence is, at least, Jewish and biblical. The Christian, under pain of heterodoxy, must accept both the Old and the New Testament as inspired by God. What does it mean, then, to proclaim as divinely inspired the books where Yahweh rules fearfully not only to fight but to exterminate whole populations so as to end the suffering of the faith of his people Israel?

Of course, if it is admitted that the violence in the Bible becomes sinful when the biblical context progressively changes, one can sidestep this by saying that what was previously held to be imperative, the New Testament has declared to be sinful. But the problem of moral relativism reemerges more poignantly than ever before. Is it true that all societies' contexts change at the same time, equally? If so, will not Latin America be in a context closer to that of the Old Testament than of the New? It is tremendously frightening to imagine that *what may be imperative in Latin America is sinful in Europe*.

Therefore, the Bible, with its rediscovered historical relativism, may not seem to be any longer the fitting principle to establish clear and univocal norms. On moral questions, the magisterium prefers more often to appeal to *nature*. It supports itself by a certain natural law of *things*—implicit in the mechanisms and causes that are observed repeatedly in nature. It certainly alludes to this when it discards violence for necessarily producing greater reactions, violence, and evils than those it pretends to remedy.

Consequently, in broad terms, everyone is aware that the evolution of the human species—because we understand the historical ages and bring to them paleontological data—has shown, if not that evolution is based on violence, at least that the exercise of violence was universal in the past and then ever so slowly diminished. This evolution can be imperceptible within a generation, or rather within the era dominated by our experience, but it is undeniable when we consider long periods of time. Every modern civilization is situated on past violence, and this contradicts the principle of a spiral, where each use of violence would beget a greater violence. Few (I believe) would dare to erase the French Revolution (if some kind of time machine would allow them to travel into the past) on the pretext that the growing evils carried by that violence overshadow by far the good brought on by the democracy that arose from it.

In other words, when we seek a norm that suggests a clear yes or no concerning the use of violent means—or even when we try to find a line that ethically separates the good and the evil in the more or less violent means we could use in the struggle for justice—we find that reality is very complex. And the norms are therefore more relative or more dependent upon that complexity.

That is why the bishops are quite classical in their theology concerning the moral norms for the use of violent means. These norms do not depend on an abstract, univocal, and immutable principle. They do depend on an *intricate web of conditions,* like those enumerated by classical theology to judge whether a war was just or unjust.

In order to see to what point the norm is thus relativized, one of the conditions for the just war was the pragmatic norm of being able to win it. And here we find the same caution when we are told that we must consider "the totality of the circumstances" and, among them, "the risk of provoking foreign intervention, no matter how legitimate it may be" (Medellín, *Conclusions,* II:16).[19] It will be said that this approaches political amoralism. What happens, once again, is that seeking moral truth (*Gaudium et Spes,* 16) has been shown to be more difficult than it seemed.

We thus finish with this special problem (far from being the only one) and return to the larger question treated in this third point. How far have we gone in this problem? In my view, we have proved once again that there is no specific necessity that leads from analysis of the class structure to political amoralism. Precisely when it is experienced, directly or indirectly, that the use of certain means—praised by Marx "in the middle of the last century"—would constitute today "simplifications . . . which, abstracting from specific essential factors, prevent any really rigorous examination of the causes of poverty" (VII,11), not only do Christians modify that analysis but also the majority of Marxists (even Lenin himself) have to do so.

Why does the document insist that, in the analysis that focuses preferentially on class struggle, "any reference to ethical requirements . . . makes no sense" (VIII,7) and that "the very nature of ethics is radically called into question" (VIII,9)?

I believe that, in principle, this is due to a misunderstanding. The document seems to believe that the conditions that give rise to class conflict in society *relativize* the *absolute* truth to the point of taking away its character. There is some confusion here that—after what has been said about the Enlightenment—is very dangerous. It has to do with *identifying absolute truth with total truth*.

Total truth is impossible within history; but that does not mean that everything is relative. To struggle against the relativity that proceeds from all the elements that condition our approximations of truth does not mean we are not getting closer to truth itself. Those successive approximations form part of an infinite dynamic, just as the Truth we humbly approach is infinite. So to admit the social conditioning of truth—like any other conditioning of it—is not the same as amoralism or the negation of the transcendence of theoretical or ethical truth. It does mean that we are seeking such truth; and experience, foresight, and comparison help us not to "betray the poor" whom we intend to serve (XI,10).

On the practical level, however, one cannot deny that liberation theology must face specific commitments where it is difficult to make clear distinctions. And this is not because liberation theology may undertake or be allowed to undertake a Marxist analysis but because, once any truth-seeking analysis of reality is undertaken, Christian moral *rules* do not seem clear enough to determine definitely what the spirit of the norm indicates.

I have before me an article. From its authorship, it could be said that it stems from liberation theology—if everything that liberation theologians say must be categorized as such. In any event, the article states that the process of liberation in Latin America takes place through the guerrilla wars that have been fought in the different countries of the continent, such as Brazil, Peru (is it referring to the best-known guerrilla group, the *Sendero Luminoso?*), Uruguay, and many others. It should be made clear beforehand that I have no doubts about the orthodoxy of the theologian in question. Nor do I think he may be a victim of political amoralism and even less that that judgment comes from a logical necessity inherent in a Marxist analysis. It does not lead me, nevertheless, to agree with him. I believe there is an error in the article (and I have tried to explain it elsewhere), because I understand that a prolonged guerrilla war has effects perhaps more destructive of the social ecology than a war between countries. First of all, it is false that violence began with guerrilla warfare. On the other hand, guerrilla warfare should not be initiated without an awareness of what experience teaches about its consequences. And war cannot be valued *solely* by the intention to seek justice, nor by the disinterest and courage of those who commit themselves to the poor to the point of undergoing torture and death.

But much remains to be said. There are at least three distinct conflicts and only the individual person to face them. There is the global conflict—those who assume the cause of the poor and those who fight against it. There is also the conflict between those who accept and do not accept (for moral and, at the same time, practical reasons) what tactics can and cannot be used in that struggle so as not to prejudice those who are served. And finally, there is the theological conflict, perhaps the most profound one, where one also must choose sides.

It is easy (perhaps too easy) to say that on each one of these levels one can make the right distinctions. But once one has taken a general position, the distinctions are easily lost or overlooked. And if, out of fear, one makes conditions out of these distinctions, one may end up taking a position opposed to what one originally sought.

With reference to the last level—the theological—will I end up choosing what the magisterium of the Church uses to combat the theology of liberation (or "certain aspects" of it as the practical negation of the Christian faith), disassociating myself from both colleagues and friends, and proving that I have not fallen into their errors? Is it possible and realistic to defend liberation theology without acknowledging that it has defects that can be identified? How does one make distinctions in such a way that the nuance could be effectively recognized but at the same time remains *only* a nuance?

I would also like to refer very briefly to the painful moral situations of Christians, submerged as they are (like it or not) in that type of conflict. Not long ago, a Uruguayan guerrilla leader died in the prison where for many long and terrible years he had been serving his sentence in an exemplary (so far as can be known) manner. He seemed to have much blood on his hands. Certain politicians invited Christians to attend the burial of this dead "companion." With whom, with what, does one enter into solidarity? With the values or intentions of guerrilla warfare, beginning with its methods? With the values shown by this man, a victim of the terrible violence who valiantly underwent prison, torture, sickness, and death—whatever had been his past? To decide in this case, for the majority of people, means to take up a cause, unfamiliar to those outside of it, without being able to explain it or nuance it. Photographs were taken of those who attended the funeral. Those who were not there will always be conspicuously "absent" from the photo. No one can escape what that might mean in the uncertain future.

I would ask those in the Vatican who compose this kind of document to make an effort to understand. Do not condemn moral indecision or assume that the lines between good and evil have been erased in the complex and always unsatisfactory judgments that Christians—as well as Marxists—have to make when facing this kind of problem (whose solution always appears as terribly *relative*). In fact, the more relative and insufficient it may appear, the more moral it may be.

This truth is evident, especially among the young, when after seeing what takes place in class struggle and what justice demands, they join a cause, often without having a sense of that relativity. They begin to employ certain means that seem effective and good— at least, provisionally good—and when they do not see tangible results, they feel the temptation not so much toward violence for violence's sake but toward an unexpected escalation of means. It is true that on that path one might arrive at the "systematic and deliberate recourse to *blind* violence, no matter from which side it comes" (XI,7).

The question is not whether this should be condemned; probably the whole world, including the genuine Marxists, would agree it should. The problem is how to attack evil. I believe one thing is clear: the evil is not in doing an analysis of the class system or in doing it from a partisan praxis. It is in *not having another education or other moral principles* beyond the results of such an analysis. Does this happen with Marxists? In some, it is possible; in all of them, no. However much the Christian—who has a spiritual tradition that helps one in a deeper way to think about and evaluate the means used—might succumb to political amoralism, it would be absurd to attribute this to Marxist analysis and its "internal logic." It is very possible that someone might be led to unsound judgments; but this is not due to the analysis but to the difficulty of grasping every nuance in complex situations that may appear to be very simple.

4. Finally, we find that the relativization of truth, according to the document, applies to what can be identified primarily with absolute Truth: the very faith of Christian revelation. Here, the document clearly supports the "logic" that has been evident throughout the preceding paragraphs.

In sum, the analysis of reality in terms of class struggle can be inadequate; but in and of itself it does not have any limits. According to the document, no area, not even the highest—the religious— escapes it: "The fundamental law of class struggle has a global and universal character. It is reflected in all the spheres of existence: *religious, ethical, cultural, and institutional.* As far as this law is concerned, *none of these spheres is autonomous.* In each of them this law constitutes the *determining element*" (VIII,8).

This loss of autonomy in areas where the absolute truth of revelation is primary would seem utterly unacceptable. And even more so if, in place of autonomy, that truth was *determined* by the same partisan element we have been following here: the praxis of class struggle.

We have already seen the problem this poses for an ethic that would like to maintain "the transcendent character of the distinction between good and evil" (VIII,9). But this goal is then translated or, rather, transmitted to the "theological" area. "A radical politicization of faith's affirmations and of theological judgments follows inevitably from this new conception" (IX,6)—"politicization," not in the sense that the political consequences of faith and theology are multiplied or exaggerated but rather (as has been demonstrated before with regard to ethics) in the sense that theological judgments and the expressions of faith are relativized and become results and not causes. In effect, "the question no longer has to do with simply drawing attention to the consequences and political implications of the truth of faith, which are *respected beforehand for their transcendent value.* In this new system, every affirmation of faith or of theology is *subordinated* to a political criterion, which in turn depends on the *class struggle,* the driving force of history" (IX,6).

However, before moving on to the theological plane where this relativizing subordination shows—according to the document—its most negative aspect, that of a *Church of the people,* it is necessary to examine one point in the previous argument.

Partisan praxis, epistemological partiality, relativization of truth, relativization of theology and of faith: these are the logical steps that the document has, with more than enough emphasis, sought to trace.

But, it is important to point out that among liberation theologians there are *some* who have expressly denied the logic of the *last step.* The use of the analysis employed by the social sciences would go *up to* the subject matter of theology. The latter has its own specific criteria and would not then be subordinated to the hermeneutic relativization emanating from the analysis of "reality." The question, then, is one of having recourse to social analysis as a way of understanding a situation, and not as a way of studying theological subjects.

But in my opinion it is not possible to raise this epistemological barrier and leave the social sciences at the threshold of theology. A purely logical connection, however, does not allow condemning a theology as heterodox on the pretext that making an erroneous statement would be more logical if that statement, in reality, was not made. The most that the magisterium can do, then, is to warn of the possible danger. But, making allowances for this possible misunderstanding, I believe it is still necessary to accept the challenge that the document makes here, and it stems from any kind of analysis of the social conditions of knowledge—and not only from Marxism.

A *first* observation: the weight of the argument that the document develops is more on the evil consequence than on the evil foundation of the analysis of reality. It seems not to be important whether the analysis is faithful to the real situation that is analyzed. If, from link to link in the argument, this analysis ends up relativizing faith and theological judgment, then it is to be false. But the document itself, perhaps without realizing it, enters into a type of analysis that, without being explicitly Marxist, leads to similar conclusions.

The final "Orientations" of the document begins by stating that "the warning against the serious deviations of some 'theologies of liberation' must not at all be taken as some kind of approval, even indirect of those who keep the poor in misery, who profit from that misery, who notice it while doing nothing about it, or who remain indifferent to it. The Church, guided by the Gospel of mercy and by the love for mankind, hears the cry for justice. . ." (XI,1). And earlier in the Introduction, the document had given similar notice: "This warning . . . should not at all serve as an excuse for those who maintain an attitude of neutrality and indifference in the face of the tragic and pressing problems of human misery and injustice."

In the two texts just quoted, the analysis of society uses *class interests* as its key and points out the different degrees and mechanisms of those interests. The fact that this analysis does not use *scientific* or *ideological* terminology does not fool anyone. It is an excellent analysis and exposes complicit interests that often are disguised, like those that appear under the guise of neutrality or indifference.

What is the purpose of that analysis? It is to prevent what is already a defective interpretation of faith that uses as a "pretext"—and so deforms it—"theological judgment" and the expression of "faith" that this document purports to represent. That defective interpretation of faith would be at least as great a deviation as the defects pointed out in the "theologies of liberation."

The one thing that is missing in the document is to generalize the hermeneutical principle it uses as if it had arisen from pure common sense: the position one takes in the class struggle affects one's ability to understand correctly (to read correctly) the Word of God. This Word is, without a doubt, from the viewpoint of the document, absolute Truth; unfortunately, the individual whom the document describes as not "doing the truth" is not free to properly listen to that Word. Therefore, suggests the document, continual vigilance is required, a constant conversion and a continual "preferential option for the poor," in order to get closer to that absolute Truth that is revealed to us and questions us.

A *second* observation: It is necessary to note that this hermeneutical dependence is not the equivalent of determinism. Or at most it is equivalent to a determinism that is only relative, in other words, to a conditioning or a pre-conditioning. As in the previous example, it does not relate to something necessary that is imposed on truth and is above it. I have already indicated that a simplistic version of Marxism holds that in analyzing the social class to which a human being belongs, one already knows how that person will think and what importance he or she will have in history.

That approach to the problem of epistemological conditioning is clearly false, even for intelligent Marxists—so false that, if it were true, Marx would never have been able to write what he wrote— socially conditioned as he was. Rightly, whoever holds a theology of the Spirit that leads to truth and, little by little, to "all truth" (Jn 16:13) does not have any reason to fear that class position may be *determining* his or her mentality and preventing a further approximation to a richer and more correct reading and interpretation of the Word of God. I believe that, to evaluate what the Enlightenment has meant for theological hermeneutics and for post-conciliar theology and exegesis in the Catholic Church, a theology of the Spirit is necessary—a pneumatology with which this document seems entirely unfamiliar or which, at least, it does not integrate with the criteria whereby liberation theology should be judged.[20]

To understand the mechanism of this hermeneutical role of "praxical" justice, or rather, to place it on the *true* side in the conflicts that provoke the domination of some human beings by others, it is necessary to understand its limits. The document seems to suggest that the theological criteria, including obedience to the magisterium, are subordinated to parameters that proceed a priori from one's position in the class struggle, this time introduced within the Church itself: "The partisan conception of truth, which can be seen in the revolutionary *praxis* of the class, corroborates this position. Theologians who do not share the theses of the "theology of liberation,' the hierarchy, and especially the Roman Magisterium, are thus discredited a priori as belonging to the class of the oppressors. Their theology is a theology of class. Arguments and teachings thus do not have to be examined themselves since they are only reflections of class interests. Thus, the instruction of others is decreed to be, in principle, false" (X,1).

Again, painfully but frankly (what other recourse is there?), I believe that the magisterium itself is discredited by this regrettable caricature. I am not an assiduous reader of everything that liberation theology produces. I cannot be, because I have work to do in it, and that means being at the service of Christians who are reflecting on their faith. I can not, for the same reason, affirm that no one has said something similar to what is charged. However, I can affirm by oath that that *is not* liberation theology.

How does this proceed, then, if a portion of the Church that shares "the earthly lot of the world" (*Gaudium et Spes,* 40) manifests some theological idea, some understanding of faith that seems not to have the same preferential option for the poor that the Church *as a whole* has made its own? What happens if the principles held as the expression of the Christian faith are not applied or are not effective in their application?

Short of giving up theology and short of judging the Church as itself *outside the faith,* what the reasonable theologian must do is raise a question. He or she does not criticize the Church a priori, nor does the theologian assert that, because it is said that the Vatican controls great wealth, its thinking *must* be in favor of the rich and the oppressors. What remains for the theologian—contributing to the continual and necessary purification of the Church (*Gaudium et Spes,* 43)—is to review the Church's *own* theology and abide by the criteria of faith as they come to us through Christian revelation and tradition. The theologian (who is not a poet nor a politician) exists to do that scientific work. It is clear that this option does not signify an impossible neutrality. As the document states, in the face of the poor, neutrality is false. But it is not the appearance of how an idea or theological judgment fits into the option for the poor is worded

that determines its theological value. Its value comes from the fact
that the foundation of that interpretation has been reexamined.

What the document credits to the theology of liberation
(although it may be very little)—"restoring to a place of honor the
great texts of the prophets and of the Gospel in defense of the poor"
(IX,10)—springs precisely from having suspected that much theology had spiritualized, individualized, and deviated from that biblical teaching. It did not declare such theology false beforehand. It
sought, with the most serious exegetical tools, the literal sense of
those passages and "discovered" what today the Church unan-
imously values.

* * *

And so I end this long, critical reading of the second part. I do not
pretend to have covered each and every one of the paragraphs that
make up the five chapters. But I have discussed the majority of
them. I have followed what seemed to me to be the clearest and most
logical path that would bring to light a single and ordered argument,
which otherwise was not easy to discern. I also say the "better"
paragraphs because, from each and every step taken, I believe valu-
able observations may be drawn to improve, to clarify, and to nuance
the theology of liberation that we practice. In terms of the theological status of these chapters, the reader will recall that that was the
subject of the first paragraph of this chapter, before beginning the
critical reading.

Of the paragraphs of the document not covered by this inventory
reading I can say little. The final sections of the document seem to
have sought to tie up all the loose ends. Some of what is written there
is so deracinated that I confess to not understanding what it means.
For example, in the "Orientations" one finds a small *list* of theological elements that the " 'theologies of liberation' . . . tend to misunderstand or to eliminate, namely: the transcendence and gratuity of
liberation in Jesus Christ, true God and true man; the sovereignty of
his grace; and the true nature of the means of salvation, especially of
the Church and the sacraments" (XI,17). I suppose, by the use of a

word like "transcendence," that some of these items have been treated already in the first part and reappear here only as a summary.[21] I have no idea why others are placed here. Finally, I do not see what others could mean, at least when they are applied to liberation theology.

Not being able to touch upon everything, I also leave aside the denunciation of certain real or presumed abuses. It may be true, for example, that the Eucharist may be transformed into "a celebration of the people in their struggle." I have not had the opportunity to witness this transformation. I do not know if the document is referring to the language that is used or if it is dealing with a theological notion, in which case I do not see that the struggle for justice (if that is what is meant) requires any transformation to be celebrated as a work of grace in the eucharistic thanksgiving if you can use this redundancy.

Lastly, there remains a subject that, strictly speaking, would seem to belong to this chapter but that will be treated in the following one: the subject of a *Church of the people* or a popular Church.

I say that it would seem to belong to this chapter because it could be said (and I believe the document sees it this way) that it is one more instance of how the analysis of the class struggle, introduced within the very reality of the Church, divides it into a Church of the poor and a Church of the rich.

"The 'theologies of liberation' of which we are speaking, mean by *Church of the People* a Church of the class, a Church of the oppressed people" (IX,12). "The Church, the gift of God and mystery of faith, is emptied of any specific reality by this reductionism. At the same time, it is disputed that the participation of Christians who belong to opposing classes at the same Eucharistic Table still makes any sense" (IX,8).[22]

As long as this is a specific case within the general question analyzed here, I do not see that it demands a special development. On the other hand, I believe that the phenomenon of the *popular Church* is too significant to subsume under what is treated in this chapter.

4

POPULAR CHURCH, POLITICAL CHURCH

The question of the *popular Church* or the *Church of the people* cannot be reduced merely to being the ultimate consequence of a particular analysis of reality—in this case, Marxist. Among other reasons, on the Latin American scene, this Church has rightly been called "of the people," not because liberation theologians have baptized it with that name after creating it but because it arises out of the popular culture itself. Now, Marxism certainly does not belong to the "people" in Latin America, nor does it belong to what could be called the urban working class, much less to the native cultures (constituting the majority in some countries, or important enclaves in others). Like any European ideology, Marxism remains a phenomenon of the middle class.

Having said this by way of introduction, this chapter will briefly study the interpretation—profoundly political—that the Vatican document makes of this significant ecclesial reality. It is significant not only and not so much for its large membership but, above all, for having introduced important modifications in liberation theology itself—modifications that the document (following its predetermined line of interpretation) seems to ignore.

From this specific case of the popular Church, and going back to what was studied in the previous chapter, I will set forth my own interpretive hypothesis of the entire second part of the document, just as I did at the end of the first part.

The Church and Popular Movements

It is relatively easy, as I have tried to show in the last few pages of the previous chapter, to interpret, as if it were the final consequence of the analysis of class struggle, the birth of a popular Church as the interjection of sociological analysis into the theological and supernatural theology of the Church.

So we read: "Class struggle . . . divides the Church" (IX,2). "The *Church of the poor* signifies the Church of the class" (IX,10). "The 'theologies of liberation' of which we are speaking, mean by *Church of the People* a Church of the class" (IX,12). It is not strange, then, as has already been indicated, that this *reduction* of the Church to being "a reality interior to history" may be considered as "the gift of God and mystery of faith, [which] is emptied of any specific reality" (IX,8).

It is of more interest to me to examine the historical basis upon which the document works regarding the origin of the popular Church. It is my opinion, founded on a study I did on that origin, that the document would have gained much in the understanding of that phenomenon by reducing to *two* theologies the plural form that it uses to designate the "*theologies* of liberation." In effect, between those two theologies, during the beginning and middle of the seventies, the *Church of the people* appeared and developed as a new phenomenon in Latin American ecclesiology.

During those years, from causes that are extraordinarily difficult to reduce to a common denominator, a considerable mobilization of the poor and the marginalized occurred. What is unique is that, with only occasional religious or political charismatic leadership, some urgency or possibility within the small religious or social sphere that these people occupied led a segment of the population that had previously seemed passive and resigned to create its own models of organization and mobilization.

At times, this brought about a populist political party or (if one prefers to avoid that sometimes pejorative term) a party "in the manner of the people." Sometimes the Church gave them a place—unique in times of dictatorship—to meet, reflect, pray, or worship. Generally, these movements lacked, at least at the beginning, a particular ideology. Often the process of mobilization and the force of circumstances itself—more powerful than abstract ideas—led these movements to exercise some option on the social or political plane, although at other times they remained neutral.

Speaking in general, it is extremely difficult in Latin America for the religious element in its most vague sense—touching upon the whole gamut from deep and committed reflection on faith to syncretism and superstition—not to be in some way present. Moreover, apart from exceptions that are perhaps becoming more numerous, this religious element is linked to the religious organization par excellence that the Latin American people have known for centuries: the Catholic Church.

That is why popular mobilization has often been made real *on the ecclesial level or principally on that level,* no matter what its cause: a political victory like that of Peronism before the last military coup in Argentina; the Sandinistas in Nicaragua; the countless varieties of base communities which arise above all to express religious needs; or periods in which political activity becomes difficult and means are sought to put into effect human rights or land ownership—to name a few.

In other words, and independent of any value judgement, the Church—which has been accustomed to having small active minorities and large, inert, and silent majorities—is facing a new phenomenon: a considerable popular mobilization within its own walls.

Something should be added that has significant value for the present study. Without going into too many considerations that would be beyond the scope of this book, it is necessary to add that actually the official Latin American Church is clearly approving this popular mobilization, without distinguishing its theological orientations. Without a doubt, there is a certain triumphalism or, rather, a definite optimism when it is seen that, within a general process of secularization, suddenly hundreds and thousands of groups spontaneously approach the Church and become active and enthusiastic members.

One of the primary ambiguities of this popular Church and its base ecclesial communities is that the whole world is busy counting them, yet no one has any interest in knowing what makes them so appealing. There is an interest in taking advantage of them, no matter what the motivation or the consequent praxis. If they have defects, one should suppose that they are in the process of improving. Not many pastors (there are some) deprive themselves of this small and possibly ephemeral ecclesial triumph, because they suspect there may be some danger—such as that expressed in the document.

In any event, contrary to what that document presupposes, liberation theology—and Marxist analysis, even less—has had little or nothing to do with the origin or growth of a *popular Church*. In a first stage, motivation and mobilization arose from the spontaneity of the people. That is the source of the expression *born of the people,* which is theologically ambiguous but sociologically correct.

The theology of liberation—as a theology that stems from and is the product of learned classes—reached this common and poor people at a second stage: as a reflection on the *existing* praxis. This does not minimize its importance. Liberation theology assumed this new reality within the reflection on faith, and defended the capacity of the people *to be Church* without having to change cultures or classes, much less their religion, and to take on an ecclesial responsibility. The theology of liberation also called attention to the fact that, in the past, the Church had often followed the easiest road: teaching without listening.

The historical description of the phenomenon does not end here. Many questions remain to be answered, and many doubts can be raised. But some elements, already present here, are worth highlighting because they are absent from, or have not been well understood by, the document being analyzed here.

As has already been said, the existence and justification of the Church that has arisen from this popular mobilization *does not stem from* any kind of social analysis. Moreover, just as by its ethnic and cultural origin that "people" is very different from the "proletariat" (of Marx), so an analysis of class seems incapable of encompassing the richness and strength of the Latin American popular element. That is why to continue such analysis relative to the ideological and oppressive elements in the religion that the people practice seems to be an estranging and elitist undertaking—an undertaking of middle-class groups who wish to think for the people without joining and understanding them.

In summary, this second tendency of liberation theology—as far as it has made the people (already mobilized or on the road to mobilization) not only its immediate object but already its principal *subject*—has been separating itself from the social sciences (and their analysis), from politicization (as a hermeneutic element), and finally, from Marxism.[1]

For the same reason, I have wanted to separate the specific subject of the treatment of theological hermeneutics in the last paragraph of the previous chapter. For one who lives and works in Latin America, it can only be a gross error—certainly spread by the mass media—to pretend that the phenomenon of the "Church of the people" (or the appearance of countless base ecclesial communities, to be more exact) is the final consequence of the use of the Marxist analysis of class struggle. On the other hand, the document, as a rule, does not deal with exaggerations or caricatures. Must we conclude, on this particular point at least, that the document is based on a lack of serious information? Or that it derived its information from the reading of some journalistic work and so confused the real facts?

That may be the case, but the key lies deeper. I believe this because several facts, which may be considered small or isolated in themselves, point to a more exact knowledge than has been common about the popular Church that, nevertheless, is accused of being defective. In any case, these negative aspects *do not* come from the analysis of class struggle.

Thus, the document recognizes the "religious," nonclassist, and in principle nonconflictive origin of the popular Church. Nevertheless, it persists in saying that its danger consists in betraying "the religion of the people in favor of the projects of the revolution" (XI,17). Who would be the *betrayers?* Obviously, the Marxists would be; yet, in an immediate way, so also would the liberation theologians and the pastors who inspire the people, and who divert religious energy toward the "politicization of existence." In point of fact, says the document, they alone can be accused of "misunderstanding the entire meaning of the Kingdom of God and the transcendence of the person" (ibid.).

If I am not mistaken, the document is very conscious of the fact that the popular Church is not the work of liberation theology but of the spontaneous religiosity of the people themselves; it recognizes further that their religiosity is no longer that which, thanks to Marxist analysis mixed with faith, led the faithful to recognize class enemies within the Church. However, the document fears that a Church thus formed may be *manipulated,* "betrayed" by those who at the same time manage religiosity and undertake a political analysis of reality.

The base ecclesial community seems to be, in itself or in principle, a place where the people themselves practice an analysis of their own praxis. If the people do this, how then can they be "manipulated"? That is an ambiguity from which the document cannot escape and which it does not attempt to clarify. Nevertheless, if the people with their liberating praxis use their own *praxical words* and even teach something to theology, it is clear that they are already the subjects, and not the mere objects, of their own history. Their historical strength must stem from the fact that, more or less consciously, they know where to find and how to combat the mechanisms of their oppression.

Yet, on the other hand, is it not understood that this is a "conscientizing" (consciousness-raising) process and that, to carry it to a successful end, a change of cultural and educational structures is needed? Is the base ecclesial community always or in some cases a "conscientizer," for example, of its own religious ideas, or are its members already "conscientized"? In any event, where does one obtain the criterion by which to judge the degree of that "conscientization" and yet not manipulate the community? This real ambiguity, which can be read in the works of liberation theologians, is found in two paragraphs in close proximity in the document.

First one reads: "They pervert the *Christian* meaning of the poor,[2] and they transform the fight for the rights of the poor into a class fight within the ideological perspective of the class struggle. For them, the *Church of the poor* signifies the Church of the class which *has become aware* of the requirements of the revolutionary struggle as a step toward liberation and which celebrates this liberation in its liturgy" (IX,10; latter emphasis is mine). On the other hand, although it may seem to say the same thing about class struggle, it does not say the same thing about the consciousness of the people two paragraphs later: "But the 'theologies of liberation' of which we are speaking, mean by *Church of the People* a Church of the class, a Church of the oppressed people whom *it is necessary to 'conscien-*

tize' in the light of the organized struggle for freedom'' (IX,12; emphasis mine).

It may be that this ambiguity is resolved in the very process by which the base ecclesial community teaches the poor about the kingdom of God. Yet something happens here that cannot be attributed simply to the development of Marxist analysis and that certainly points to something typical of this second tendency in liberation theology, aimed at the people: "For some [theologians] the [oppressed] people . . . become *the object of faith*"(ibid.).

The object of faith indicates (for this document) a way of following the religious-conscientizing path of the people within the base ecclesial community that is, if not totally a-critical, nevertheless raised to the level of an almost absolute truth. That is why it is not strange that absolutizing that path may appear to the document to be the immediate preparation for denying the authority and particularly the magisterium of the official Church that wants to place conditions on any faith expression of the Church of the people.

> Building on such a conception of the Church of the People, a critique of the very structures of the Church is developed. . . . It has to do with a challenge to the *sacramental and hierarchical structure* of the Church, which was willed by the Lord Himself. . . . Theologically, this position means that ministers take their origin from the people who therefore designate ministers of their own choice in accord with the needs of their historic revolutionary mission (IX,13).

In all these descriptions, elements from the class struggle are intermingled that (except for posing a hypothesis that I will later examine) do not correspond to reality as I know it, with perhaps one exception. However, it cannot be denied that by painting this picture of the popular Church, the document gives expression to a dual sentiment: that of the hierarchy thinking it is losing its grip on the Church of the people; and that of the people who feel the hostility and incomprehension of some priests/pastors and who do not distinguish between political authority that can be changed in principle if not through dialogue, and an immovable ecclesiastical authority (see IX,13).

I believe that, after this examination, it is possible to reject most of this description—because it is inexact, exaggerated, or because it is simply not representative. But it can no longer be pretended that the document's view of the popular Church stems only from an abstract reason about what should logically be the final consequence of using the analysis of class struggle.

If we add to this description the obvious allusions to the conversion of the Eucharist into a "celebration of the people in their struggle" (X,16; see IX,10), one can not but believe that, at this point of describing the *popular Church,* we face a phenomenon that is much more practical than purely theological: the experience of *concrete and recent* conflicts between the Holy See and Latin American ecclesial realities where the former has seen its authority diminished. Whether or not they have a direct relationship with liberation theology, the churches of Nicaragua and Brazil (and as I will try to show, the church of Cuba) constitute the key to understanding how the document, without naming them, treats the problems which concern them.

Manipulation of the Popular Church?

It is relatively easy to prove that some Latin American countries in particular pose more pointed questions than others to the universal hierarchy of the Church. It is not a daring hypothesis to suppose that an echo of those difficulties and concerns colors the pages we are studying.

I am deceiving neither myself nor anyone else if I center those difficulties on two countries where the phenomenon of a *Church of the people* (as the document calls it) appears most clearly and with more visible political consequences: Nicaragua and Brazil.[3]

The journeys of His Holiness to those countries—together with some events that singularly marked those occasions—as well as the difficulties of some theologians with the Congregation for the Doctrine of the Faith and the political positions of some priests and bishops—all explain Rome's concern. It was certainly not unexpected that a document directed to all of Latin America and to subjects strictly related to its problems would carry the stamp of serious Vatican concern to put an end to certain variances and ambiguities—not only theoretical but also practical, and directly experienced at that always-painful point where politics and religion meet, as it were, jealously looking at one another.

Moreover, when I speak of variances, I realize that, because there are no uniform criteria to judge them, their discernment is an especially delicate matter. I do not mean that the authorities of the Church, and particularly John Paul II on his trips, say contradictory things. Yet they do give great importance to differences and nuances that no one else perceives with the same clarity. I believe this is reflected in the document, and I will try to demonstrate it.

We begin with a country that, because of its geographic dimensions and the qualitative and quantitative importance of its episcopacy, should occupy an equally sizeable place in ecclesial concerns: Brazil, which, furthermore, is one of the countries that most clearly manifests the presence of a growing popular Church.

Why is this Church concerned? Because of an interconnected group of causes; the majority of them have appeared in some way in the criticisms that have just been discussed about the Church of the people. Others, although tacit, are easy to imagine because they are closely linked to the description and the judgment that is made of the popular Church.

The *first* reason, in my view, comes from the fear that arises from any spontaneous popular mobilization, especially in Latin America and in relation to the Church. The analysis that Medellín made about institutionalized violence, at the end of the sixties, today falls short. The temptation of counter-violence—given that the primary violence is a clear and continual seed of revolution—is associated in the long run with any popular mobilization. It is the *people* who are the victims of that institutionalized violence. In such a case, it is impossible to see what might check the progress of Marxism, its promises, and the idealistic attraction it can have. It would not be the first time that something that begins as a spontaneous popular movement within the walls of the Church becomes, *lacking any other effective outlet,* Marxist—with or without the help of liberation theology. International capitalism, for example, is enough to bring about such results.

The difficulty of stopping, or even slowing, a popular movement once it has begun must have been experienced by John Paul II when, speaking in a São Paulo stadium to metal workers of the region, he exhorted them to defend their rights yet without entering into the class struggle. Even supposing that those workers would have understood what he meant—i.e., "do not modify structures but rather convert individuals to respect the transcendence of persons and defend your systematically ignored rights, through the only means at your disposal, the union"—they would have returned the next day to the class struggle and to the possibility that it might entail (finding no other solution) an escalation of violence.[4]

A *second* reason for fearing the development of a Church of the people in Latin America is the relative indifference of the people toward ecclesiastical authority in general and its magisterial function in particular. The middle classes have a more serious view, although in many cases it is fairly magical, of the importance of orthodoxy (whether it be of liberation *or* of salvation—if this distinction means anything). The ordinary people, on the other hand, although they may externally respect ecclesiastical authority, do not understand the majority of its decisions on doctrinal or sacramental matters. The Holy Father may have experienced something of this during his stay in Nicaragua, and the document's allusions prove the importance of that traumatic experience.

It is important to point out that the Church of the people shows great affection, respect, and reverence with regard to the authority of its pastors. That, at least, is the Brazilian experience. This may be, however, if not fortuitous, at least fragile. It depends in good measure on the extraordinary leadership ability that many of their pastors have. The authority of the bishops is personal. It does not depend on their office as such. Yet the tendency in the naming of new bishops in almost all of Latin America (choosing them precisely for their uniformity and conformity to Rome's orientation more than for their charism of leadership) foreshadows the fact that in the future the new episcopate will lose a large part of its present ability to contain and direct the popular Church. It presages bad days for the ecclesiastical hierarchy that will have to face popular mobilization. What we know of Nicaragua indicates that this is already happening there.

However, I believe that these two reasons give way to a *third* and primary reason: the danger of manipulation. It may be that this point separates me, in some way, from one or another of my Latin American colleagues, but I cannot help but think that, sociologically speaking, this characteristic internal weakness must be recognized. On the other hand, it is enough for the present discussion to say that Rome *might* think this way. In any event, the people are spontaneously mobilizing themselves. It is difficult for this spontaneity to be connected profoundly with the Christian faith—if one understands by profundity not feeling but reflection.

I believe it would be unrealistic to ask the masses (often without any instruction) for a political conscientization that will run parallel to a deep knowledge of Christian faith and its consequences for the problems of life. Furthermore, the most elementary realism would add that the daily urgency of the struggle for survival does not leave room (even if there were the intuitive capacity or intellectual formation) for such reflection.[5] Without reflection, it is difficult to resist the easy solutions—of understanding, if not of attaining them—that are proposed. Because of my familiarity with the base ecclesial communities, I know three influences that, to a certain degree, may be called *manipulative*—in the sense that they further the (Christian) reflective progress of the community.

Church authorities are familiar with and use one of these influences. As far as the Church has political or economic power, it can for a period of time maintain its attractiveness and therefore its authority over popular communities that have all-embracing needs. There is, for example, a "pastoral plan of the land" that is not so much pastoral as it is "political," in the good sense of the word, where religious motivations form a constitutive part of the demands for land reform.

One must recognize, *second,* that wherever there are such popular communities in the Latin American continent, people from other social classes offer services that the community itself cannot. Among those services is the one that the theologian can provide, if he or she accepts being the "organic intellectual" of those communities: representing them, giving them some foundation for their inter- and extra-ecclesial demands, providing for them the fundamentals of a conscientization that is appropriate to their possibilities of knowledge and analysis of reality.

There is no doubt that liberation theology, in its simplest and most basic forms, plays an important and, in some extraordinary cases, decisive role in satisfying these needs. My conviction is—considering the seeming accusation by the document of giving bread before giving the Gospel—that to confront the urgencies and possibilities arising from the needs of the people, one should take (more than the development of faith and its consequences) the shortcut of teaching them to analyze reality.[6] I have already indicated why, in principle, one should not be alarmed that this analysis introduces elements that, rightly or wrongly, are called Marxist. The theologians I know are well aware of the precautions and the nuances that are needed so as not to stray from the truth. However, those very nuances do not always reach all of the members of the base communities.

Third, specific political manipulation must be added to this. Politicians, whether on the electoral or revolutionary level, do not fail to see that the spontaneity of the people, above all when they are found to be partially mobilized, is a precious element that can be used as a lever for large-scale sociopolitical changes.

Anyone who can, furthermore, present a reality favorable to those people with the corresponding *pathos,* as is the case with Marxists, will not find any "enlightened" resistance in the people, precisely because of their ideological weakness and lack of deep reflection on faith. This is even more the case when they feel that the domain of the sacred is confined to traditional religious feelings and ceremonies, while Marxism reserves for itself the domain of profane history where the revolution takes place.

This is what must be recognized if one wants to understand the version, whether true or false—or probably both—that Rome holds about what is happening in Nicaragua.[7]

And this is what allows for an understanding of several apparent paradoxes. One is that the relations of the Vatican with Cuba may appear much more normal than those it maintains with Nicaragua, whereas everything should make one believe that the opposite would be more logical. Cuba is an officially Marxist-Leninist country. The Cuban authorities do not allow the existence of a popular Church in Cuba, nor the development of that theology of liberation that is supposed to be allied to Marxism; the only liberties that the Church in Cuba enjoys are limited to what has been called (in similar situations) the "sacristy," that is, to the church grounds. There is no Catholic teaching in the elementary, secondary, or university schools, whether public or private.

In other words, between the two—Nicaragua and Cuba—the former, even assuming that it may be a communist country, should come first in terms of the sympathies of Vatican diplomacy. But this is far from the case. That is because of the mistaken belief that the comparison *favors* Nicaragua. When I mentioned that Cuba was an unavoidable reference point, I meant precisely the fact that, from the viewpoint one must have in order to understand the second part of the Vatican document, Cuba is the exemplary case in Latin America. It is the only Latin American country where Marxism appears as it should be and the only one that obligates the Church to limit itself to only one activity, also conceded as what it should be: the clear and unanimous opposition.

The argument is equally valid for Nicaragua—and potentially also for Brazil—as the most dangerous country in the eyes of Vatican diplomacy. And the central religious element used to define such dangers is the existence of a strong popular Church.

It will be said that this is to "reduce" the principal criterion to the political and to set aside the pastoral and the religious. But one must not forget that that is precisely the impression that dominates the reading of the second part of the document: the fact that Marxism is absolutized as *the* "political" incarnation of evil, as something whose "core" is constituted by "atheism and the negation of the human person, his liberty, and his rights."

The same interpretive observation is valid for those apparent ambivalences to which I have already referred. The Supreme Pontiff, in an emotional statement in Ayacucho (Peru), urged and demanded that the guerrillas of the *Sendero Luminoso* make peace and put down their guns. He did not, when he visited Nicaragua, urge or demand the same thing of the *contras* who—officially supported by the United States—fight against the state and the Nicaraguan people within and outside its borders. The same ambivalence may be recognized in the phenomenon of hundreds of priests who continue exercising their ministry despite their holding high-level military posts, and who are in the paid service of South American dictatorial governments, officially carrying the ideology of national security (which the Church condemned at Puebla) to the citizens in military service. When it is said that there is no parity in these examples, it is forgotten that in one, and not the other, of these cases absolute evil is perceived.

It will be said that this politicizes the Church. Doubtless this is not true in principle, just as it is not true that there is an alliance between the Vatican and certain lines of international politics. But it does lead to the tacit assumption that others—a kind of secular arm —may assume political tasks that the Church cannot assume.

Unlike the time of the Council—shortly after a cold war ended— the Latin American Church is entering another cold war, with its consequent Manicheism. Although it may not seem so, this politicizes the Church, perhaps more than ever before in this century, because only on one side of that war is an absolute evil detected.

What is considered as important and what often, in this second part of the document, I have called the resentment toward Marxism that is presented with bitter and unjust exaggerations, is nothing else than the *pathos* with which Christians have had to face Marxist regimes, a pathos born of what such Christians consider to be the culpable misunderstanding of those who take elements from Marxism and become involuntary accomplices in its destructive task.

By Way of Summary:
A Warning to the Church at Large

At the beginning of this book I promised myself to take seriously the expressions of concern that constitute the *Instruction On Certain Aspects of the 'Theology of Liberation'* and to make the closest possible reading of it. I do not know if I have done so, but I do not think I am being disloyal in saying that was what I intended. If perhaps I have not done so, it is because it honestly has not been possible.

I believe it to be a pledge of seriousness to have tried to give to a document that explicitly attempts to be negative, the greatest negative force possible, above all in its first part. Instead of analyzing (and even less of discarding) argument by argument, I believe I have arrived at a systematic view of the theology that opposed liberation theology and that saw in it, generally speaking, a grave deviation from the Christian faith.

It was not very difficult to arrive at this systematic level because I believe that the first part of the document is very logical. It brings to its final consequences, without fear of seeming out of date, a clear, anti-secularist intention: the same intention that defines liberation theology as the reduction of the Gospel of salvation to an earthly gospel. Cardinal Ratzinger himself helped in the understanding of that systematization when, in the previously quoted interview in the *Osservatore Romano,* he opposed the faith to "the affirmation, in the West, of the new 'tertiary bourgeoisie' with its liberal-radical ideology which is individualistic, rationalistic, and hedonistic."

In this context (which if it is not Latin American, is culturally familiar and intelligible to us), one can understand the resurgence of a theology that seeks, by discarding all immanent activities, a powerful return to the relationship of the individual with a transcendence that is critical of that developed bourgeois mentality. That theology finds the solution in the individual spirituality which is linked to the transcendence of the person, an individuality that is in no way "individualistic" in the sense of "selfish," but sincerely ready to unite such transcendence with a certain option for the poor and for justice.

If, nevertheless, I cannot accept that the theology of liberation I know has to be condemned, it is for two closely united reasons, the first of which is negative and the second, positive.

The first reason is that for presenting liberation theology as immanentist—the principal argument to which Cardinal Ratzinger's mention of context points—the document is obligated to attribute to liberation theology a distinction and a separation that is expressly denied by the *central* theological core of that theology. In the addendum to the second chapter, I pointed out how there can be no liberation theology for me without the full understanding of the declaration of the Council of Orange about the supernatural beginning of faith in its widest sense, reaffirmed by the Second Vatican Council, which adopted, with different words, the supernatural existential of Karl Rahner.

The second reason: in liberation theology, which can no longer be disassociated from the most orthodox Catholic theology, *history* can no longer be separated from *the human place where the individual encounters transcendence.* Another thing will be, as the Council also says, that one will have to distinguish whatever may be defined as historical progress from what in history is construed as truly transcendent, in the already active presence, though mysterious, of the Kingdom of God among us.

Fidelity to that magisterium does not allow me to treat the theology of the *Instruction* as heterodox. I heartily grant to others the right that is denied to me—to fashion, with that theological opinion, an enriching theological pluralism, like the one that Karl Rahner postulated shortly before his death. However, I am obligated by fidelity to the most solemn magisterium of the Church to deny that there is a transcendence proper to the individual that does not extend to the history wherein people seek to give to society more just and congenial structures.

This first part of the document, perhaps the richer part, forces the reader to take that part as a whole, expressly because of its theology, and to make a global judgment of it. That is why it is not possible to take single elements from it to counterbalance a nuance that is lacking or a gap that may occur in the theology of liberation. The fact that one may take it or leave it speaks in the document's favor, despite the fact that it may lead some to think that the document is not valued at all because it is not taken as "improving" the theology of liberation itself.

Another thing happens (almost the opposite) with the second part. The context from which it proceeds, insofar as the reader may imagine such a context, is a strange world, very different from that of the first part of the document. It is strange because it seemingly springs from factors whose coordinates are ignored and which, in turn, ignore essential elements of Western culture, such as the Enlightenment. It is also strange because it seems to know only the issue, posed in the form of a dilemma, *Marxism or nothing*. In other words, either all of the values that are sought within history lead to Marxism or, to avoid that, it is necessary to empty Christianity and place it outside the world. It would be enough to add that the document does not understand by Marxism what is commonly understood by that word in the West: a cultural influence, perhaps in decline. Rather, it understands it to be a rigid official system and, above all, a political system.

In this conflict, intensified by a large dose of resentment or, perhaps better, a theology dependent on a politics without hope, we Latin Americans do not recognize our reality nor even the European reality that underlies the first part of the document.

Nevertheless, this does not stand in the way (and this is a little paradoxical) of the fact that this second part, theologically weaker, less nuanced and balanced, and systematically sloppier, may perhaps be more useful. Perhaps because it is more political and therefore more concrete, it calls our attention to the realities that we could and should improve. There are ambiguities like those that often creep into our judgments or attitudes with regard to the popular Church or to the very use of that expression for all kinds of very different realities. There are classist exaggerations in our conception of the Church, its function, and its possibilities. There is the simplistic use of categories dependent upon the class struggle for the explanation of any phenomenon of oppression. I believe that liberation theology is sufficiently strong and mature to recognize many of these things without diminishing their value.

A final observation about the whole of the *Instruction:* Let no one be deceived into thinking that only Latin American theology is involved here. If the analysis I have made is correct, the two parts, despite their differences, are united by one point that affects the entire Church: *the negative evaluation of Vatican II and of the postconciliar period.*

In the first draft of this small work, I brought together quite a lot of material that I planned to accompany each theme, providing quotations (without reference to the author so as not to involuntarily compromise anyone) from major theologians—European as well as North American—showing how their theology is opposed to that of the *Instruction*. And vice versa. But I did not want to break a lifelong rule: citations without naming their authors. I prefer that only my own thoughts run the risk they deserve on a subject such as this, which I believe affects everyone.

One of the functions of the Synod of Catholic Bishops called for November, 1985, will be exactly that of evaluating the two decades since the closing of Vatican II. The whole Church, not only Latin America, must know what that means and what will happen there. It should know in what theological, pastoral, and political context this issue will be posed (whether in the Synod or in the ongoing daily life of the Church). These pages have been written to show just that context, within the framework of liberation theology.

These pages will have fulfilled their task if they convince the reader of the necessity to reaffirm the solemn magisterium of the Church which, after so long a time of immobility and absenteeism, returned, as Paul VI said, to place the Church at the service of humanity. This book will have achieved its purpose if it convinces the reader that the implementation of the Council has not gone too far; that, on the contrary, it has been blocked midway in its journey. Finally, this book will have been worth the effort if it shows that the same Spirit who helped the Council speak the truth also helped it to speak clearly. Fidelity to that Spirit does not allow *the opposite* to be spoken on the pretext of explaining the Council better or of preventing it from being misunderstood. If this occurs, then this book will achieve its goal. In case of doubt, it will always be better to wager on what Cardinal Henri de Lubac expressed in a prayer: "If I lack love and justice, I separate myself completely from you, God, and my adoration is nothing more than idolatry. To believe in you, I must believe in love and in justice, and to believe in these things is worth a thousand times more than saying your Name."

AFTERWORD

Since the writing of these pages, two important events bearing on our subject have occurred in the Church. The Extraordinary Synod, convoked to evaluate the aftermath of Vatican II, has been held. And the "positive" document promised in the "Instruction on Certain Aspects of the Theology of Liberation" was issued the Easter following the publication of the *Instruction* (1986).

The reader might well wonder how these two events modify the theological panorama sketched in the foregoing pages. It would probably be an oversimplification to say that they do not modify it at all. On the other hand, there is no getting around the fact that not only does the new document take back nothing of the first, but the Sovereign Pontiff himself, in his letter to the Brazilian bishops, explicitly reiterates his approval of the first document, which, the letter goes on to say, is of a piece with the second. Anyone who knows the earnestness and consistency of Cardinal Ratzinger knows how unlikely it is that he has changed his theology. And that theology, if I interpret correctly, condemns central features in the theology of liberation as we know it today.

There is, however, a new element in the second document. I think we have the necessary tools for evaluating it in this book. The reader will recall that in my commentary on the first document I pointed to something positive in its very negativity. In the first document the condemnation of liberation theology generally renounces any appeal to "common theological sense." Instead, after presenting an overly schematic or summary view of the theology of liberation, it condemns it via an appeal to another theology—which latter, this first document is at pains to emphasize, is accepted by many theologians, and even representatives of the ordinary magisterium of the Church. But this "theological honesty," as I termed it in chapter 1 of the present volume, carried a price tag. As far as we can gather from what we know about what went on in the Synod, that body gave up hope of achieving any unanimity on the theology from which the first document condemned certain aspects of the theology of liberation.

Now, I think everyone is aware of Pope John Paul II's declared intent, manifested in so many different ways, especially on his visits abroad, to bind the Catholic Church together in a unanimity that will lend it renewed strength and vitality. With this in mind, we may very probably conclude that the first document, while it enjoyed the personal approbation of the Sovereign Pontiff, now appeared to him to "go too far" in its condemnations, at least too far to be practical. To put it another way, it was not that the first document was judged erroneous or even exaggerated; it was only that now it was regarded as inopportune to impose it or to insist on its imposition when it was not supported by unanimity in the area of episcopal collegiality.

At all events, it is clear that the second document returns to what we have called common theological sense. Anyone can see this by going through it with an eye for the huge number of citations that pepper it, from Vatican II to Medellín to Puebla to the recent encyclicals on the social doctrine of the Church. The propositions cited are obviously deemed known and accepted by all. By contrast, there is very little by way of theological disquisition. In other words, the second document no longer endorses the theology through which liberation theology was condemned in the first. Now the aim is unanimity—with the tacit admission, therefore, that a pluralism exists to which the first document would like to close its eyes.

The press has seen in this second document a retreat from positions taken in the first. It likes to cite a phrase from the letter sent by the Sovereign Pontiff to the Brazilian bishops in which it is declared that the theology of liberation is "not only useful, but necessary."

Regarding the matter with greater precision and impartiality, however, I think that we must recall the context in which this phrase appears:

> To the extent that it represents an effort to find these right answers—answers that will be steeped in a grasp of the rich experience of the Church in your land, answers that will be as effective and constructive as possible, while at the same time in harmony and consistent with the teachings of the Gospel, our living Tradition, and the perennial Magisterium of the Church—we are convinced, you as well as I, that the theology of liberation is not only fitting, but useful and necessary.

As we see, the Sovereign Pontiff—who refers to his own thinking on this theology as stated in the first document, published "with my explicit approbation"—judges that the Brazilian bishops, whose thinking he knows to be different from his own, may permit the development of a certain theology of liberation on condition, however gently implied, that that theology conform to the teachings of the papal magisterium.

As a Spanish theologian has written, we may regard the most positive thing about the second document to be the fact that circumstances have, as it were, obliged it to be written. It will not stuff the bells—it will not make it possible to pretend, as some seem to wish to do, that "nothing has happened here." Taken together, the two documents are a call to reflect on what is actually at stake. How can you have a wholesome, evangelical *theological* unity in a Church where not all think the same, but where, I think we may safely say, all seek the truth with equal sincerity?

Thus, I believe that what was written in the foregoing pages retains its intended value of service to the cause of a dynamic unity that will send us all down the road to "the whole truth," accompanied by the spirit of Jesus.

Montevideo, May 8, 1986

NOTES

Chapter 1: The Key to Reading This Book

1. This procedure, furthermore, puts many of us Latin American theologians in a painful situation. We had to choose between separating ourselves from our colleagues and friends by criticizing extremes that seemed unacceptable to us, or forming a common block with them to attack what, objectively speaking, seemed to us (as a method of evaluation) an exercise in bad faith. To ponder the difficulty of this choice, one must recognize a factor that, disgracefully, has escaped the Congregation: excessive or not, liberation theologians in Latin America do not take advantage of their prestige or their positions as professors but rather risk (because of what they understand to be the demands of their faith) more important things that can lead, in extreme cases, to the risk of life itself.

2. The only reaction made public by a bishops' conference comes from Peru. It is significant that in their response, in spite of working in Rome and under the co-leadership of Cardinal Ratzinger himself, and widely quoting the Vatican document, the Peruvian bishops did not want to cite the paragraphs in which liberation theology, or certain forms of it, was condemned as the practical negation of faith. Neither did the Peruvian bishops condemn, as was asked of them, the theology of Gustavo Gutiérrez.

3. The first paragraph of Chapter IX, about the "Theological Application of This [Marxist Ideological] Core," is very significant. It states there that "the positions here in question are often brought out explicitly in certain of the writings of 'theologians of liberation.' In others, they follow logically from their premises." And so that there will be no doubt about its universal scope, the paragraph ends by saying, "We are facing, therefore, a real system, even if some hesitate to follow the logic to its conclusions. As such, this system is a perversion of the Christian message as God entrusted it to His Church. This message in its entirety finds itself then called into question by the 'theologies of liberation.'"

4. In reality, it is hard to see how, logically, a *risk* or *danger* can be condemned as "damaging." While it remains only a risk, it is not damaging and, because it has passed through many trials, it may often be healthy for avoiding the error. These and other similar flaws make it difficult to recognize in the document the precision in the use of terms

and arguments that we are accustomed to seeing in the works of Cardinal Ratzinger.

Chapter 2: Liberation and Secularism

1. Returning to the case of Gustavo Gutiérrez, this explains why, despite the fact that he showed evidence that his theological work does not contain "concepts uncritically borrowed from Marxism" or "a biblical hermeneutic marked by rationalism," the observations made by the Congregation for the Doctrine of the Faith about his theology (in private, of course, although later they may be published or made known) were not retracted, as classical Christian morals would seem to demand. The fact is that the core of the Congregation's negative evaluation was not there (as will be seen in what follows).

2. Speaking of this *opposition* that we find in the document, we refer to the way in which it proceeds—its argumentative structure: "One thing is dangerous for the other." And this is already an opposition. Explicitly, on the other hand, the document systematically denies that there is or should be opposition—and even accuses the theology of liberation of introducing such opposition. In reality, it has to proceed in this way so as to be able later to accuse (with a minimum of logic) liberation theology of being left with only "profane," "temporal," or secular elements. A critical reading will allow the reader to decide if indeed the *document's* theology is not the one which introduces an opposition (between the terms that liberation theology unites) in order to be able to favor only the "religious" (sin, word of God, and faith *versus* ideology, urgency, earthly impatience, and so on).

3. *Gaudium et Spes,* n. 4, is much more exact and presents a perfectly coherent exegesis when it attributes the *discernment* of the signs of the times to the historical sensitivity of the individual and attributes its *interpretation* to the light of the Gospel (see the expressions of the "Message to the People of Latin America" from Medellín).

4. According to Luke, however, Jesus' answer to the interpreters of the Law and God's revelation (whether God or Beelzebub was responsible for the cure of the possessed) would also play a part. See Lk 11:14; Mk 3:22-26.

5. That is why asking for a "sign from heaven" may be associated in Matthew with wickedness and *idolatry:* "An evil, faithless [or rather, idolatrous] age is eager for a sign . . ." (Mt 16:4). The very fact of

not seeing God's victory in the liberation of one possessed (no matter who may be the direct agent of that liberation) because it is supposed that God can have a criterion different from the welfare of the individual, is to badly interpret the Bible, and consequently the Gospel (see Mk 3:22-29; 2:23-3:5; Lk 10:25,37, e.g.).

6. At least in Luke's version, with his respective "woes." This version simply cannot be ignored, even if its authenticity may be questioned.

7. See the "Woe to you rich" and the "impossibility" mentioned by Mark (10:24-27), which alludes to the one exception: *de potentia absoluta,* or the infinite power of God.

8. "It is significant that the option for the young has in general been passed over in total silence" (VI,6).

9. On the other hand, Moses says to Pharaoh, "Let *my people* go" (Ex 5:1, Elohist version).

10. As von Rad notes, it is precisely the Priestly Code that refuses to employ the term "covenant" on various occasions related to Sinai. On the other hand, exegetes argue whether *the reason Moses gives to Pharaoh* so that he would let them leave Egypt—celebrating a cult of Yahweh in the desert—manifested a sincere intention or whether it was tactical. In any event, to credit Moses with the intention of establishing the cult of the Covenant on Sinai is going too far. The cult would be nothing more, according to the story, than a "sign" (Ex 3:12; the exegesis of this sign is what is discussed here), that is to say, a step into the larger plan of Yahweh which everywhere seems related to the previous sociopolitical situation of slavery and to the future sociopolitical situation of the promised land as an independent Israel.

11. Since I have not seen the use of this kind of argument in the works of Cardinal Ratzinger, I think it is necessary to question (it is certainly important for theological qualification) the degree to which the document truly corresponds to his thought.

12. It is interesting to note that the phrase "our Lord Jesus Christ [who] made himself *poor* though he was rich" confirms what we have said—that the Gospels never use the term "poor" to designate the detachment of Jesus or of his disciples. Therefore, the document is limited to quoting Paul's phrase (2 Cor 8:9). What is even more interesting is that although it uses the verb form "made himself poor"—and not the noun "poor"—it does not refer to material poverty but to that metaphorical poverty (self-imposed) that Philippians 2:7 calls the "emptying" (kenosis) of his divine condition. The "poverty" of Jesus is

metaphorical as is the last part of the sentence: "so that you might become *rich*."

13. This is the expression used by the Latin American magisterium at Medellín: "We also, the new People of God, cannot cease to feel his *saving passage* in view of 'true [sociocultural] development, which is the passage for each and all, *from conditions of life that are less human, to those that are more human*'" (*Conclusions*, Introduction: 6). "All *'growth in humanity'* brings us closer to *'reproducing the image of the Son'*" (*Conclusions*, IV:9).

14. Once more it is necessary to understand that this orientation does not stem from—nor pretend to lead to—indifference in view of the existing evils in history or a *laissez faire, laissez aller* attitude in view of the oppression of the poor by the rich (see IV,11).

15. Here too it should be made clear that the document never forgets that its markedly religious conception has "consequences" on other levels, including the sociopolitical one: "However, the *Letter to Philemon* shows that the new freedom procured by the grace of Christ should necessarily have effects on the social level" (IV,13).

16. See *Conclusions*, II:1.

17. So as not to understand this to imply a disdain for interpersonal relationships, the final words are: "Moreover, since charity is the principle of authentic perfection, that perfection cannot be conceived without an openness to others and a spirit of service" (IV,15).

18. As indicated previously, it seems extremely significant that these central and decisive words would be conspicuously absent from the only Latin American episcopal document (from the Peruvian Bishops' Conference) that I have seen with regard to this subject.

19. Although this is not the place to extend this pronouncement to my colleagues, friends, and collaborators, it is easy to infer my thoughts in this regard from what has been stated.

20. It manipulates it, accepting or rejecting its dictates according to a "political criterion" (IX,5).

21. Of course, as the reader will understand, this "identification" that was denied before gives rise to new criticisms. They may be worthy of consideration, but logically they cannot be the same ones that arose from the supposed "separation" that was previously attacked. As a text opposed to this "identification," *Lumen Gentium,* 9-17 is quoted. Note, however, the contrary meaning of *Lumen Gentium,* 16. Only on this occasion the internal logic of this passage and the following ones in the document makes preferable the Spanish version (often very bad), which, instead of "God himself makes history," reads "God is made

history'' (or rather, perhaps, ''God makes himself history'') in an explicit allusion to the Incarnation. The reason for this preference is, then, that when ''history becomes a central notion,'' John's old statement that ''the Word became (or is made) *flesh*'' can be translated by ''God is made *history* (history being the essential characteristic of human ''flesh''). The following paragraph (IX,4) is clear enough when it keeps speaking of ''identifying God himself with history.'' That is also why in the next phrases I speak of the Incarnation as the theological base for the search for transcendence *within* history and not outside it.

22. This is in contrast to Rudolf Bultmann, for whom the life and death of Jesus constitute an absurd destiny and reduce, therefore, the encounter with the transcendent to the existential interpretation of what happens with the "Jesus of faith" in the heart of each person. Therefore it makes no sense—unless we are dealing with the rhetorical device used by Aeschines against Demosthenes (*On the False Embassy*)—to accuse liberation theology of overly depending on none other than Bultmann! In the document there is a veiled reference to this dependence (without indicating where it is concretely manifested) in the position attributed to liberation theology of opposing—again using the same argumentative device—"the *'Jesus of history'* and the *'Jesus of faith'*" (X,8).

23. That human history cannot be said to be purely "immanent" (as the document does) is proved by Matthew 25:31ff. What one does for one's neighbor, *even without religious consciousness (see Mt 25:37,44)* results in justification, not as a reward but as an effect, in the kingdom of God. Therefore, following the same principle recalled in *Lumen Gentium,* 16, something that is intrinsically related to the Kingdom cannot, without theological error, be called *immanent* (cf. X,6).

24. This is not the proper place to study in detail the innovative doctrinal richness of Vatican II, especially *Gaudium et Spes*. Here I am giving some references so the reader may compare statements and draw his or her own conclusions.

25. As will be seen, all the allusions point to it. If only the conciliar theology, represented by *Lumen Gentium,* were represented, then the rest of the pontifical discourse would be meaningless. It is important to point out that this closing homily initiates the theological considerations of the Second General Conference of Latin American Bishops in Medellín (see *Introduction*:1).

26. Paul VI understands that the theology of the Second Vatican Council belongs to what is called the "ordinary magisterium" of the Church, although in this case it is the *solemn* exercise of that magisterium. The

reason for this is that Vatican II did not want, unlike other ecumenical councils, to anathematize what was considered opposed to orthodoxy. With all due respect to this option (as novel as the very teaching method employed by the Council), I believe that the distinction between ordinary and extraordinary magisterium is not based on a difference between literary genres. I understand an ecumenical council, to which is attributed a "doctrinal richness" referring to faith and/or customs, to belong to the *extraordinary* magisterium of the Church, whether or not it has canons and whether or not it condemns dogmatic errors. However, even if this were not the case, the obligation to adhere to the "doctrinal richness" of an ecumenical council cannot be compared to adherence to what comes from the Congregation for the Doctrine of the Faith, which is subordinate to the Council.

27. It is clear that there are always exceptions, like that of baptism of desire (and the like) but their very conditions make them exceptional. The vast majority of humanity lived and acted seemingly outside of that divine and saving reality, on the level of "pure nature," unelevated and incapable, therefore, of doing anything valid for the transcendent and divine.

28. I said "anticipated" because, although the term "supernatural existential" could have been already known (I do not know exactly when Malevez began to work theologically with his idea), Karl Rahner did not at that time accept the wider interpretation of the *initium fidei* or the preparation for faith, proposed by Malevez. He would accept it later, perceiving its truth at the same time as that doctrine converged with his concept of the concretely supernatural existence of every person.

29. Note that we say "compartmentalization," and not conceptual distinction, because the supernatural existential of Rahner—although it excludes from the real history of humanity a time, or a group, or persons deprived of *grace*—does not confuse grace or gift from God with nature in general or with the "pure" nature of the individual. This is still a necessary concept for understanding that grace is precisely that: grace, gift.

30. *Gaudium et Spes* is equally clear on the subject: "In wonder at their own discoveries and their own might men are today troubled and perplexed by questions. . . ." (3)

31. Weekly English edition, December 2, 1984. It is a conversation between Cardinal Ratzinger and the Italian writer Vittorio Messoni—a conversation that was the basis for Ratzinger's book *Reporte sulla Fede,* published May 30, 1985, by Edizioni Paoline.

32. Practically all the points in the summary of the interview, where Cardinal Ratzinger sees negative elements at the present time, are closely related to explicit conciliar themes. It is hard not to see that he feels, at least implicitly, that the Council itself went too far and that today the Church is suffering the consequences.

33. So as not to be accused of taking this statement out of context, I should add that the text from 1 Timothy 2:4-7 is then cited: "God, our Lord, wants all people to be saved and come to the knowledge of the truth," which, he immediately adds, consists in knowing that "God is one, that there is only one mediator between God and humanity: the person of Jesus Christ, who delivered himself up for the redemption of all."

Chapter 3: Liberation and Hermeneutics

1. It may be read in this way, but I believe that it would be a mistake. In the fourth chapter, I hope to be able to show why and in what sense— even referring to Latin American realities—the whole document, including its second part, constitutes a "warning to the Church" in its entirety.

2. See my address, "The Shift within Latin American Theology," given in Toronto on March 22, 1983, and published by Regis College, Toronto. An article containing the French translation of that address was published in *Etudes* 361 (Paris, 1984), pp. 149-161.

3. "Different" does not mean "independent," as North Atlantic theology almost systematically assumes it does. The human problem of the developed person is vitally linked to that of the oppressed person because we are dealing with two sides of the same coin, or two defects of the same "structure." That is the reason, perhaps, for the anti-Marxist animosity of much "developed" theology that prefers to think of its problems as independent.

4. Note that—if it is true that this quote from Paul VI stems from countering the temptation to "accept elements of Marxist analysis without recognizing their relationship with the ideology"—the result is that it accepts, not so much the determinism or the materialism or the atheism, but the "totalitarianism" to which the so-called Marxist governments have accustomed us (although to varying degrees)—only to be equalled or bettered by other "totalitarianisms" which, on the periphery of capitalism, are called anti-Marxist and sometimes even Christian.

5. A logical error is unleashed here, improper in a document from the hierarchy such as this one. After stating that this disassociation is "impossible," it concludes: "That is why *it is not uncommon* for the ideological aspects to be predominant." What would be uncommon would be that the impossible could be common.

6. What one cannot do is put "the deviations and risks of deviation" (Introduction) on the same level as something that would be "damaging" to the faith.

7. Moreover, the document would have to "recall" that, according to Vatican II, atheism is not an originary phenomenon—that is, that no one is an atheist for the simple desire to be so. The rejection of God always stems from causes, whether good or bad, that are closer to the individual. Furthermore, as noted earlier, the Council committed itself to seriously studying the true causes of atheism—although this has been quickly forgotten. I believe that forgetting this is even clearer with regard to Marxist atheism; in the document, at least, there is not the least effort to know or indicate what would be the reasons for its atheistic position.

8. This is the reason for Marx's criticism of the "materialists" (mechanicists) of his day—even of Feuerbach. It is enough to carefully read Marx, substituting the term "realist" for "materialist" to understand that "material" cannot be equivalent to "non-spiritual." The historical reason that explains Marx's predilection for the term "materialism" instead of "realism" seems to be that "realism" meant a conservative and naive return to a gnoseological posing of the problem prior to idealism. Neither must one exclude a certain strong urge to, literally, "*épater le bourgeois.*" On the other hand, one must not forget that the conditioning of ideas by the economic means of production does not imply materialism, because Marx continually mentions the "spiritual" elements of the mode of production, or rather, the human relationship that all productive labor imposes.

9. See, for example, St. John Chrysostom (*In Ep. I ad Tim.,* ch. IV, hom. XIII): "God, in principle, did not make some poor and others rich, nor at the moment of creation did he give more treasures to some than to others, but rather he left everyone the same earth that they might cultivate it. [That is why] no one can, without injustice, make himself rich." Or Pseudo-Clement of Rome (*Recognitiones*): "All things in this world were meant for the common use of all; nevertheless, one unjustly called this, his and the other, his, from which originated the division among mortals." According to St. Ambrose, "avarice deter-

mined the rights of ownership" (*In Psalmum CXVIII,* sermon **VIII,** 22).

10. See Leo XIII's entire argument in *Rerum Novarum,* 17 and 19.

11. On this point, the resentment that so often disgracefully appears in the document—detracting from its credibility—reappears, provoking a small theological reversal (or at least an irony): "The universality of love of neighbor and brotherhood become an *eschatological* principle, which will only have meaning for the 'new man' who *arises out of the victorious revolution*" (IX,7). It is clear that if the classless society is the work of the victorious revolution, it is a result immanent in history and is not, by that fact, an eschatological principle. If this quotation expresses Marxist thought and not that of the document, it is even more unfortunate because I do not think any Marxist would qualify the revolution as an eschatological principle.

12. Will the document count among those factors Marxism with its struggle of more than a century to awaken the consciousness of the oppressed? Not doing so, does it gain, or lose, credibility?

13. The synoptic Gospels—Matthew contains a whole chapter of the most powerful and varied castigation by Jesus of his enemies (Mt 23)—do not describe any reconciliation between Jesus and his enemies. It would seem, then, that this is not how Jesus understood love of one's enemies.

14. One of the most original, though less known, characteristics of liberation theology is its "interclassist" character. The class enemy, which is the middle class for the poor working class, is not treated as an enemy in the Latin American church but rather is called to dialogue and persuasion. And it has responded in an incredibly positive way. The vitality of the Latin American church before the advent of popular movements or communities came from a middle class that opted for the poor. The theology of liberation, like it or not, began in that middle class and was a catalyst for it. Without the preparation of the global Church by that middle class, the popular movements and communities either would have arisen without leaders or would have progressed without allies and support. It is paradoxical that Marxist logic would be judged harsher than that which leads Christians to opt for a class that is not their own, for the class enemy, objectively speaking.

15. I would like to present, especially on this point and those that follow, something that should already have been made clear: although at times general observations may be made about the criticism of the document, I am committing myself alone, and if I speak of liberation theology, I understand by it that which I have developed, taught, and

practiced. I feel and maintain my total solidarity with my colleagues who pursue, so I believe, the same line of theological thought. However, *I do not speak for them.* I speak only for myself. I want to say this because in this and in the following chapters I will admit that certain criticisms or warnings made about liberation theology are well founded. I do not know if my colleagues would admit them in the same way. But a document like the one studied here questions my own faith and on this point, more than any other, *amicus Plato sed magis amica veritas.* (May Plato forgive me.)

16. The context, while the text may be ambiguous, seems to suggest that the Church should be a Church of "the poor" yet not *reduced* to only the proletariat and even less to their political interests.

17. See Pius XI's encyclical *Nos es muy,* to the Mexican people on March 28, 1937. It has been argued, furthermore, whether or not Paul VI was well interpreted in Medellín with regard to revolutionary violence. Be that as it may, this is the opinion of the ordinary magisterium in Medellín.

18. Who can have such a poor memory as to forget that almost all of Europe, together with North America, in the middle of this century, suffered five years of war in which more than twelve million people died? Millions of Christians participated in that bloodbath without anyone telling them in the name of the Church to throw down their arms because the violence was not Christian. Then there were other wars—Korea, Viet Nam—and Christians took part in them, too. Why does the whole world *now* begin to ask Latin America and liberation theology what they think about violence? Latin America, for better or for worse, is a terribly pacifist continent. According to recent information, in one single region of Brazil, in the last five years ten million people died of malnutrition—almost as many as in the last world war because of violence.

19. This formulation, important for any Christian faced with this problem, is not foreign to Marxist thinkers. For that same reason, I affirm (at least in the case to which I am referring) that analysis *is nothing more than* a moment of combat and not a self-criticism of how the revolutionary process is conducted. If this is not recognized by Marxists, there is *in principle* nothing that prevents them from doing so.

20. This explains why the exegetical examples that appear in the document may give the impression of ignoring, perhaps because they are considered dangerous and divisive, the gains that have followed the distinction in biblical hermeneutics between the literary genres: form history,

redaction history, the formation of the scriptural canons and their criteria, and so on.

21. For example, I suppose that mentioning "true God and true man" with respect to Jesus Christ reflects an uneasiness that appears previously in a paragraph that says: "Of course the creeds of the faith are literally preserved, especially the Chalcedonian creed, but a new meaning is given to them" (X,9). I confess that I was not aware of this—nor is the document explicit in this regard.

22. One would expect, after all (at least so as not to offend Christian ears), that a document written by theologians would cite—even if for no other reason than to explain why it does not apply here—the all-too-well known text of St. Paul to the Corinthians. It will be recalled that he tells them they do not understand what the Eucharist is, they do not understand the Body of Christ, when they sit at the same eucharistic table and one gets drunk while the other goes hungry—doubtless because they belong to different social classes. Once more, I do not believe the document has analyzed St. Paul in depth.

Chapter 4: Popular Church, Political Church

1. It is true that in such matters, like those of the economic factors of national or international oppression, it is impossible (and the document shows this authentically) not to utilize elements that originate in Marxism, such as studying the mechanisms of international capitalism. Certainly, the social doctrine of the Church is not lacking in such elements.

2. In Chapter 2 of this book a commentary was made about the subject of poverty and the exegesis that the document does in this regard in IV, 9-10.

3. The reader may ask why Peru is not included. Certainly, it is difficult to explain the reason for the Vatican's interest in the danger that the Church in Peru may be facing. Unless I am mistaken, the popular Church there has not the magnitude and organization that exists in Brazil, nor a relationship as clear with a leftist political movement as that of the Sandinista revolution in Nicaragua. Probably, and it is sad, so much has been concentrated on Peru in an effort to achieve the condemnation of Gustavo Gutiérrez's theology. Perhaps it was thought that what this document would do on the theoretical level, a condemnation of Gustavo Gutiérrez by the Peruvian bishops, would complement on the

practical level. This does not seem to have been successful, and I am happy for one of the theologians who is most important for the whole Church today. Perhaps the pressures on the Peruvian episcopate were exaggerated and what they were prepared to do freely they did not wish to do under such external pressure.

4. It is difficult not to foresee that each time the terrible circle—democracy, institutionalized violence, subversive violence, military dictatorship, democracy—seems to be broken, it will begin again if the people, disheartened for a time in their struggle because of the repression of their rights, recover those rights again.

5. A fidelity that goes more to certain symbols and persons than to particular ideologies is a recognized characteristic of the general population.

6. In part because many Gospel notions are complex, and from this point of view, many popular communities—even using Christian expressions and images—find themselves closer to the People of God of the Old Testament.

7. I know that what I have just written about the possibility of manipulation that the popular Church presents will displease all of my colleagues. They will cite a thousand cases of profound transformation and Christian spirit in base communities, something I have not denied. It will be said that a Church in the middle or upper class is as, or more, manipulable than a popular one because of elements foreign to Christianity. Nor have I denied this, although I would add that that manipulation would utilize different means from those mentioned here and that the latter are the ones discussed in this specific case. It will be said that this is a partial and negative view of base ecclesial communities. I too have said that in this book because it is obvious: because of the document I am studying, I have to refer to the point of view, more political than pastoral, that determines the criticisms that are made and the dangers that are seen.

Imprimi Potest

William N. Addley, S.J., Provincial of Upper Canada

Toronto, April 4, 1985

Appendix

INSTRUCTION ON CERTAIN ASPECTS OF THE "THEOLOGY OF LIBERATION"

The Gospel of Jesus Christ is a message of freedom and a force for liberation. In recent years this essential truth has become the object of reflection for theologians, with a new kind of attention which is itself full of promise.

Liberation is first and foremost liberation from the radical slavery of sin. Its end and its goal is the freedom of the children of God, which is the gift of grace. As a logical consequence, it calls for freedom from many different kinds of slavery in the cultural, economic, social and political spheres, all of which derive ultimately from sin and so often prevent people from living in a manner befitting their dignity. To discern clearly what is fundamental to this issue and what is a byproduct of it is an indispensable condition for any theological reflection on liberation.

Faced with the urgency of certain problems, some are tempted to emphasize, unilaterally, the liberation from servitude of an earthly and temporal kind. They do so in such a way that they seem to put liberation from sin in second place and so fail to give it the primary importance it is due. Thus, their very presentation of the problems is confused and ambiguous. Others, in an effort to learn more precisely what are the causes of the slavery which they want to end, make use of different concepts without sufficient critical caution. It is difficult, and perhaps impossible, to purify these borrowed concepts of an ideological inspiration which is incompatible with Christian faith and the ethical requirements which flow from it.

The Sacred Congregation for the Doctrine of the Faith does not intend to deal here with the vast theme of Christian freedom and liberation in its own right. This it intends to do in a subsequent document which will detail in a positive fashion the great richness of this theme for the doctrine and life of the church.

The present instruction has a much more limited and precise purpose: to draw the attention of pastors, theologians and all the faithful to the deviations and risks of deviation, damaging to the faith and to Christian living, that are brought about by certain forms of liberation theology which use, in an insufficiently critical manner, concepts borrowed from various currents of Marxist thought.

This warning should in no way be interpreted as a disavowal of all those who want to respond generously and with an authentic evangelical spirit to the "preferential option for the poor." It should not at all serve as an excuse for those who maintain an attitude of neutrality and indifference in the face of the tragic and pressing problems of human misery and injustice. It is, on the contrary, dictated by the certitude that the serious ideological deviations which it points out tend inevitably to betray the cause of the poor. More than ever, it is important that numerous

Christians, whose faith is clear and who are committed to live the Christian life in its fullness, become involved in the struggle for justice, freedom and human dignity because of their love for their disinherited, oppressed and persecuted brothers and sisters. More than ever, the church intends to condemn abuses, injustices and attacks against freedom, wherever they occur and whoever commits them. She intends to struggle, by her own means, for the defense and advancement of the rights of mankind, especially of the poor.

I. An Aspiration

1. The powerful and almost irresistible aspiration that people have for liberation constitutes one of the principal signs of the times which the church has to examine and interpret in the light of the Gospel.[1] This major phenomenon of our time is universally widespread, though it takes on different forms and exists in different degrees according to the particular people involved. It is, above all, among those people who bear the burdens of misery and in the heart of the disinherited classes that this aspiration expresses itself with the greatest force.

2. This yearning shows the authentic, if obscure, perception of the dignity of the human person, created "in the image and likeness of God" (Gn. 1:26–27), ridiculed and scorned in the midst of a variety of different oppressions: cultural, political, racial, social and economic, often in conjunction with one another.

3. In revealing to them their vocation as children of God, the Gospel has elicited in the hearts of mankind a demand and a positive will for a peaceful and just fraternal life in which everyone will find respect and the conditions for spiritual as well as material development. This requirement is no doubt at the very basis of the aspiration we are talking about here.

4. Consequently mankind will no longer passively submit to crushing poverty with its effects of death, disease and decline. He resents this misery as an intolerable violation of his native dignity. Many factors, and among them certainly the leaven of the Gospel, have contributed to an awakening of the consciousness of the oppressed.

5. It is widely known even in still illiterate sections of the world that, thanks to the amazing advances in science and technology, mankind, still growing in numbers, is capable of assuring each human being the minimum of goods required by his dignity as a person.

6. The scandal of the shocking inequality between the rich and the poor— whether between rich and poor countries, or between social classes in a single nation —is no longer tolerated. On one hand, people have attained an unheard-of abundance which is given to waste, while on the other hand so many live in such poverty, deprived of the basic necessities, that one is hardly able even to count the victims of malnutrition.

7. The lack of equity and of a sense of solidarity in international transactions works to the advantage of the industrialized nations so that the gulf between the

rich and the poor is ever widening. Hence derives the feeling of frustration among Third World countries and the accusations of exploitation and economic colonialism brought against the industrialized nations.

8. The memory of crimes of a certain type of colonialism and of its effects often aggravates these injuries and wounds.

9. The Apostolic See, in accord with the Second Vatican Council and together with the episcopal conferences, has not ceased to denounce the scandal involved in the gigantic arms race which, in addition to the threat which it poses to peace, squanders amounts of money so large that even a fraction of it would be sufficient to respond to the needs of those people who want for the basic essentials of life.

II. Expressions of This Aspiration

1. The yearning for justice and for the effective recognition of the dignity of every human being needs, like every deep aspiration, to be clarified and guided.

2. In effect, a discernment process is necessary which takes into account both the theoretical and the practical manifestations of this aspiration. For there are many political and social movements which present themselves as authentic spokesmen for the aspiration of the poor and claim to be able, though by recourse to violent means, to bring about the radical changes which will put an end to the oppression and misery of people.

3. So the aspiration for justice often finds itself the captive of ideologies which hide or pervert its meaning and which propose to people struggling for their liberation goals which are contrary to the true purpose of human life. They propose ways of action which imply the systematic recourse to violence, contrary to any ethic which is respectful of persons.

4. The interpretation of the signs of the times in the light of the Gospel requires, then, that we examine the meaning of this deep yearning of people for justice, but also that we study with critical discernment the theoretical and practical expressions which this aspiration has taken on.

III. Liberation, A Christian Theme

1. Taken by itself, the desire for liberation finds a strong and fraternal echo in the heart and spirit of Christians.

2. Thus, in accord with this aspiration, the theological and pastoral movement known as "liberation theology" was born, first in the countries of Latin America, which are marked by the religious and cultural heritage of Christianity, and then in other countries of the Third World, as well as in certain circles in the industrialized countries.

3. The expression "theology of liberation" refers first of all to a special concern for the poor and the victims of oppression, which in turn begets a commitment to justice. Starting with this approach, we can distinguish several often contradictory

ways of understanding the Christian meaning of poverty and the type of commitment to justice which it requires. As with all movements of ideas, the "theologies of liberation" present diverse theological positions. Their doctrinal frontiers are badly defined.

4. The aspiration for liberation, as the term suggests, repeats a theme which is fundamental to the Old and New Testaments. In itself, the expression "theology of liberation" is a thoroughly valid term: It designates a theological reflection centered on the biblical theme of liberation and freedom, and on the urgency of its practical realization.

The meeting, then, of the aspiration for liberation and the theologies of liberation is not one of mere chance. The significance of this encounter between the two can be understood only in light of the specific message of revelation, authentically interpreted by the magisterium of the church.[2]

IV. Biblical Foundations

1. Thus a theology of liberation correctly understood constitutes an invitation to theologians to deepen certain essential biblical themes with a concern for the grave and urgent questions which the contemporary yearning for liberation and those movements which more or less faithfully echo it pose for the church. We dare not forget for a single instant the situations of acute distress which issue such a dramatic call to theologians.

2. The radical experience of Christian liberty[3] is our first point of reference. Christ, our liberator, has freed us from sin and from slavery to the law and to the flesh, which is the mark of the condition of sinful mankind. Thus it is the new life of grace, fruit of justification, which makes us free. This means that the most radical form of slavery is slavery to sin. Other forms of slavery find their deepest root in slavery to sin. That is why freedom in the full Christian sense, characterized by the life in the Spirit, cannot be confused with a license to give in to the desires of the flesh. Freedom is a new life in love.

3. The "theologies of liberation" make wide use of readings from the Book of Exodus. The exodus, in fact, is the fundamental event in the formation of the chosen people. It represents freedom from foreign domination and from slavery. One will note that the specific significance of the event comes from its purpose, for this liberation is ordered to the foundation of the people of God and the covenant cult celebrated on Mt. Sinai.[4] That is why the liberation of the exodus cannot be reduced to a liberation which is principally or exclusively political in nature. Moreover, it is significant that the term freedom is often replaced in scripture by the very closely related term *redemption*.

4. The foundational episode of the Exodus will never be effaced from the memory of Israel. Reference is made to it when, after the destruction of Jerusalem and the exile to Babylon, the Jewish people lived in the hope of a new liberation and, beyond that, awaited a definitive liberation. In this experience God is recognized as

the liberator. He will enter into a new covenant with his people. It will be marked by the gift of his Spirit and the conversion of hearts.[5]

5. The anxieties and multiple sufferings sustained by those who are faithful to the God of the covenant provide the theme of several Psalms: laments, appeals for help and thanksgivings all make mention of religious salvation and liberation. In this context, suffering is not purely and simply equated with the social condition of poverty or with the condition of the one who is undergoing political oppression. It also includes the hostility of one's enemies, injustice, failure and death. The Psalms call us back to an essential religious experience: It is from God alone that one can expect salvation and healing. God, and not man, has the power to change the situations of suffering. Thus the "poor of the Lord" live in a total and confident reliance upon the loving providence of God.[6] Moreover, throughout the whole crossing of the desert, the Lord did not fail to provide for the spiritual liberation and purification of his people.

6. In the Old Testament, the prophets after Amos keep affirming with particular vigor the requirements of justice and solidarity and the need to pronounce a very severe judgment on the rich who oppress the poor. They come to the defense of the widow and the orphan. They threaten the powerful: The accumulation of evils can only lead to terrible punishments.

Faithfulness to the covenant cannot be conceived of without the practice of justice. Justice as regards God and justice as regards mankind are inseparable. God is the defender and the liberator of the poor.

7. These requirements are found once again in the New Testament. They are even more radicalized as can be shown in the discourse on the Beatitudes. Conversion and renewal have to occur in the depths of the heart.

8. Already proclaimed in the Old Testament, the commandment of fraternal love extended to all mankind thus provides the supreme rule of social life.[7] There are no discriminations or limitations which can counter the recognition of everyone as neighbor.[8]

9. Poverty for the sake of the kingdom is praised. And in the figure of the poor, we are led to recognize the mysterious presence of the Son of Man, who became poor himself for love of us.[9] This is the foundation of the inexhaustible words of Jesus on the judgment in Matthew 25:31–46. Our Lord is one with all in distress; every distress is marked by his presence.

10. At the same time, the requirements of justice and mercy, already proclaimed in the Old Testament, are deepened to assume a new significance in the New Testament. Those who suffer or who are persecuted are identified with Christ.[10] The perfection that Jesus demands of his disciples (Mt. 5:18) consists in the obligation to be merciful "as your heavenly Father is merciful" (Lk. 6:36).

11. It is in light of the Christian vocation to fraternal love and mercy that the rich are severely reminded of their duty.[11] St. Paul, faced with the disorders of the church of Corinth, forcefully emphasizes the bond which exists between participation in the sacrament of love and sharing with the brother in need.[12]

12. New Testament revelation teaches us that sin is the greatest evil, since it strikes man in the heart of his personality. The first liberation, to which all others must make reference, is that from sin.

13. Unquestionably, it is to stress the radical character of the deliverance brought by Christ and offered to all, be they politically free or slaves, that the New Testament does not require some change in the political or social condition as a prerequisite for entrance into this freedom. However, the Letter to Philemon shows that the new freedom procured by the grace of Christ should necessarily have effects on the social level.

14. Consequently, the full ambit of sin, whose first effect is to introduce disorder into the relationship between God and man, cannot be restricted to "social sin." The truth is that only a correct doctrine of sin will permit us to insist on the gravity of its social effects.

15. Nor can one localize evil principally or uniquely in bad social, political or economic "structures" as though all other evils came from them so that the creation of the "new man" would depend on the establishment of different economic and socio-political structures. To be sure, there are structures which are evil and which cause evil and which we must have the courage to change. Structures, whether they are good or bad, are the result of man's actions and so are consequences more than causes. The root of evil, then, lies in free and responsible persons who have to be converted by the grace of Jesus Christ in order to live and act as new creatures in the love of neighbor and in the effective search for justice, self-control and the exercise of virtue.[13]

To demand first of all a radical revolution in social relations and then to criticize the search for personal perfection is to set out on a road which leads to the denial of the meaning of the person and his transcendence, and to destroy ethics and its foundation, which is the absolute character of the distinction between good and evil. Moreover, since charity is the principle of authentic perfection, that perfection cannot be conceived without an openness to others and a spirit of service.

V. The Voice of The Magisterium

1. In order to answer the challenge leveled at our times by oppression and hunger, the church's magisterium has frequently expressed her desire to awaken Christian consciences to a sense of justice, social responsibility and solidarity with the poor and the oppressed, and to highlight the present urgency of the doctrine and imperatives contained in Revelation.

2. We would like to mention some of these interventions here: the papal documents *Mater et Magistra, Pacem in Terris, Populorum Progressio* and *Evangelii Nuntiandi*. We should likewise mention the letter to Cardinal Roy, *Octogesima Adveniens*.

3. The Second Vatican Council in turn confronted the questions of justice and liberty in the pastoral constitution *Gaudium et Spes*.

4. On a number of occasions the Holy Father has emphasized these themes, in particular in the encyclicals *Redemptor Hominis, Dives in Misericordia* and *Laborem Exercens.* These numerous addresses recall the doctrine of the rights of man and touch directly on the problems of the liberation of the human person in the face of the diverse kinds of oppression of which he is the victim. It is especially important to mention in this connection the address given before the 26th General Assembly of the United Nations in New York, Oct. 2, 1979.[14] On Jan. 28 of that same year, while opening the Third Conference of CELAM in Puebla, Jonn Paul II affirmed that the complete truth about man is the basis for any real liberation.[15] This text is a document which bears directly upon the theology of liberation.

5. Twice the Synod of Bishops treated subjects which are directly related to a Christian conception of liberation: in 1971, justice in the world, and in 1974, the relationship between freedom from oppression and full freedom, or the salvation of mankind. The work of the synods of 1971 and 1974 led Paul VI in his apostolic exhortation *Evangelii Nuntiandi* to clarify the connection between evangelization and human liberation or advancement.[16]

6. The concern of the church for liberation and for human advancement was also expressed in the establishment of the Pontifical Commission Justice and Peace.

7. Numerous national episcopal conferences have joined the Holy See in recalling the urgency of authentic human liberation and the routes by which to achieve it. In this context, special mention should be made of the documents of the general conferences of the Latin American episcopate at Medellin in 1968 and at Puebla in 1979.

Paul VI was present at the Medellin conference and John Paul II was at Puebla. Both dealt with the themes of conversion and liberation.

8. Following Paul VI, who had insisted on the distinctive character of the gospel message,[17] a character which is of divine origin, John Paul II, in his address at Puebla, recalled the three pillars upon which any authentic theology of liberation will rest: truth about Jesus Christ, truth about the church and truth about mankind.[18]

VI. A New Interpretation of Christianity

1. It is impossible to overlook the immense amount of selfless work done by Christians, pastors, priests, religious or laypersons, who, driven by a love for their brothers and sisters living in inhuman conditions, have endeavored to bring help and comfort to countless people in the distress brought about by poverty. Among these, some have tried to find the most effective means to put a quick end to the intolerable situation.

2. The zeal and the compassion which should dwell in the hearts of all pastors nevertheless run the risk of being led astray and diverted to works which are just as damaging to man and his dignity as is the poverty which is being fought, if one is not sufficiently attentive to certain temptations.

3. The feeling of anguish at the urgency of the problems cannot make us lose sight of what is essential nor forget the reply of Jesus to the Tempter. "It is not on bread alone that man lives, but on every word that comes from the mouth of God" (Mt. 4:4; cf. Dt. 8:3).

Faced with the urgency of sharing bread, some are tempted to put evangelization into parentheses, as it were, and postpone it until tomorrow: first the bread, then the word of the Lord. It is a fatal error to separate these two and even worse to oppose the one to the other. In fact, the Christian perspective naturally shows they have a great deal to do with one another.[19]

4. To some it even seems that the necessary struggle for human justice and freedom in the economic and political sense constitutes the whole essence of salvation. For them, the Gospel is reduced to a purely earthly gospel.

5. The different theologies of liberation are situated between the preferential option for the poor forcefully reaffirmed without ambiguity after Medellin at the conference of Puebla[20] on the one hand, and the temptation to reduce the Gospel to an earthly gospel on the other.

6. We should recall that the preferential option described at Puebla is twofold: for the poor and for the young.[21] It is significant that the option for the young has in general been passed over in total silence.

7. We noted above (cf. 3) that an authentic theology of liberation will be one which is rooted in the word of God, correctly interpreted.

8. But from a descriptive standpoint, it helps to speak of theologies of liberation, since the expression embraces a number of theological positions or even sometimes ideological ones, which are not simply different but more often incompatible with one another.

9. In this present document, we will only be discussing developments of that current of thought which, under the name "theology of liberation," proposes a novel interpretation of both the content of faith and of Christian existence which seriously departs from the faith of the church and, in fact, actually constitutes a practical negation.

10. Concepts uncritically borrowed from Marxist ideology and recourse to theses of a biblical hermeneutic marked by rationalism are at the basis of the new interpretation which is corrupting whatever was authentic in the general initial commitment on behalf of the poor.

VII. Marxist Analysis

1. Impatience and a desire for results has led certain Christians, despairing of every other method, to turn to what they call "Marxist analysis."

2. Their reasoning is this: An intolerable and explosive situation requires effective action which cannot be put off. Effective action presupposes a scientific analysis of the structural causes of poverty. Marxism now provides us with the means to

make such an analysis, they say. Then one simply has to apply the analysis to the Third-World situation, especially in Latin America.

3. It is clear that scientific knowledge of the situation and of the possible strategies for the transformation of society is a presupposition for any plan capable of attaining the ends proposed. It is also a proof of the seriousness of the effort.

4. But the term *scientific* exerts an almost mythical fascination even though everything called "scientific" is not necessarily scientific at all. That is why the borrowing of a method of approach to reality should be preceded by a careful epistemological critique. This preliminary critical study is missing from more than one "theology of liberation."

5. In the human and social sciences it is well to be aware above all of the plurality of methods and viewpoints, each of which reveals only one aspect of reality, which is so complex that it defies simple and univocal explanation.

6. In the case of Marxism, in the particular sense given to it in this context, a preliminary critique is all the more necessary since the thought of Marx is such a global vision of reality that all data received from observation and analysis are brought together in a philosophical and ideological structure, which predetermines the significance and importance to be attached to them. The ideological principles come prior to the study of the social reality and are presupposed in it. Thus no separation of the parts of this epistemologically unique complex is possible. If one tries to take only one part, say, the analysis, one ends up having to accept the entire ideology. That is why it is not uncommon for the ideological aspect to be predominant among the things which the "theologians of liberation" borrow from Marxist authors.

7. The warning of Paul VI remains fully valid today: Marxism as it is actually lived out poses many distinct aspects and questions for Christians to reflect upon and act on. However, it would be "illusory and dangerous to ignore the intimate bond which radically unites them, and to accept elements of the Marxist analysis without recognizing its connections with the ideology, or to enter into the practice of class struggle and of its Marxist interpretation while failing to see the kind of totalitarian society to which this process slowly leads."[22]

8. It is true that Marxist thought ever since its origins, and even more so lately, has become divided and has given birth to various currents which diverge significantly from one another. To the extent that they remain fully Marxist, these currents continue to be based on certain fundamental tenets which are not compatible with the Christian conception of humanity and society. In this context certain formulas are not neutral, but keep the meaning they had in the original Marxist doctrine. This is the case with the "class struggle." This expression remains pregnant with the interpretation that Marx gave it, so it cannot be taken as the equivalent of "severe social conflict," in an empirical sense. Those who use similar formulas, while claiming to keep only certain elements of the Marxist analysis and yet to reject this analysis taken as a whole, maintain at the very least a serious confusion in the minds of their readers.

9. Let us recall the fact that atheism and the denial of the human person, his liberty and his rights, are at the core of Marxist theory. This theory, then, contains errors which directly threaten the truths of the faith regarding the eternal destiny of individual persons. Moreover, to attempt to integrate into theology an analysis whose criterion of interpretation depends on this atheistic conception is to involve oneself in terrible contradictions. What is more, this misunderstanding of the spiritual nature of the person leads to a total subordination of the person to the collectivity and thus to the denial of the principles of a social and political life which is in keeping with human dignity.

10. A critical examination of the analytical methods borrowed from other disciplines must be carried out in a special way by theologians. It is the light of faith which provides theology with its principles. That is why the use of philosophical positions or of human sciences by the theologian has a value which might be called instrumental, but yet must undergo a critical study from a theological perspective. In other words, the ultimate and decisive criterion for truth can only be a criterion which is itself theological. It is only in the light of faith and what faith teaches us about the truth of man and the ultimate meaning of his destiny, that one can judge the validity or degree of validity of what other disciplines propose, often rather conjecturally, as being the truth about man, his history and his destiny.

11. When modes of interpretation are applied to the economic, social and political reality of today, which are themselves borrowed from Marxist thought, they can give the initial impression of a certain plausibility to the degree that the present-day situation in certain countries is similar to what Marx described and interpreted in the middle of the last century. On the basis of these similarities, certain simplifications are made which, abstracting from specific essential factors, prevent any really rigorous examination of the causes of poverty and prolong the confusion.

12. In certain parts of Latin America the seizure of the vast majority of the wealth by an oligarchy of owners bereft of social consciousness, the practical absence or the shortcomings of a rule of law, military dictators making a mockery of elementary human rights, the corruption of certain powerful officials, the savage practices of some foreign capital interests constitute factors which nourish a passion for revolt among those who thus consider themselves the powerless victims of a new colonialism in the technological, financial, monetary or economic order. The recognition of injustice is accompanied by a pathos which borrows its language from Marxism, wrongly presented as though it were scientific language.

13. The first condition for any analysis is total openness to the reality to be described. That is why a critical consciousness has to accompany the use of any working hypotheses that are being adopted. One has to realize that these hypotheses correspond to a particular viewpoint which will inevitably highlight certain aspects of the reality while leaving others in the shade. This limitation, which derives from the nature of human science, is ignored by those who, under the guise

of hypotheses recognized as such, have recourse to such an all-embracing conception of reality as the thought of Karl Marx.

VIII. Subversion of The Meaning of Truth and Violence

1. This all-embracing conception thus imposes its logic and leads the "theologies of liberation" to accept a series of positions which are incompatible with the Christian vision of humanity. In fact, the ideological core borrowed from Marxism which we are referring to exercises the function of a determining principle. It has this role in virtue of its being described as "scientific," that is to say, true of necessity.

In this core we can distinguish several components.

2. According to the logic of Marxist thought, the "analysis" is inseparable from the praxis and from the conception of history to which this praxis is linked. The analysis is for the Marxist an instrument of criticism, and criticism is only one stage in the revolutionary struggle. This struggle is that of the proletarian class, invested with its mission in history.

3. Consequently, for the Marxist, only those who engage in the struggle can work out the analysis correctly.

4. The only true consciousness, then, is the partisan consciousness.

It is clear that the concept of truth itself is in question here, and it is totally subverted: There is no truth, they pretend, except in and through the partisan praxis.

5. For the Marxist, the praxis and the truth that comes from it are partisan praxis and truth because the fundamental structure of history is characterized by class struggle. There follows, then, the objective necessity to enter into the class struggle, which is the dialectical opposite of the relationship of exploitation, which is being condemned. For the Marxist, the truth is a truth of class: There is no truth but the truth in the struggle of the revolutionary class.

6. The fundamental law of history, which is the law of the class struggle, implies that society is founded on violence. To the violence which constitutes the relationship of the domination of the rich over the poor, there corresponds the counterviolence of the revolution, by means of which this domination will be reversed.

7. The class struggle is presented as an objective, necessary law. Upon entering this process on behalf of the oppressed, one "makes" truth, one acts "scientifically." Consequently, the conception of the truth goes hand in hand with the affirmation of necessary violence, and so, of a political amorality. Within this perspective, any reference to ethical requirements calling for courageous and radical institutional and structural reforms makes no sense.

8. The fundamental law of class struggle has a global and universal character. It is reflected in all the spheres of existence: religious, ethical, cultural and institutional. As far as this law is concerned, one of these spheres is autonomous. In each of them this law constitutes the determining element.

9. In particular, the very nature of ethics is radically called into question because of the borrowing of these theses from Marxism. In fact, it is the transcendent character of the distinction between good and evil, the principle of morality, which is implicitly denied in the perspective of the class struggle.

IX. The Theological Application of This Core

1. The positions here in question are often brought out explicitly in certain of the writings of "theologians of liberation." In others, they follow logically from their premises. In addition, they are presupposed in certain liturgical practices, as for example a "eucharist" transformed into a celebration of the people in struggle, even though the persons who participate in these practices may not be fully conscious of it. We are facing, therefore, a real system, even if some hesitate to follow the logic to its conclusion. As such, this system is a perversion of the Christian message as God entrusted it to his church. This message in its entirety finds itself then called into question by the "theologies of liberation."

2. It is not the fact of social stratification with all its inequity and injustice, but the theory of class struggle as the fundamental law of history which has been accepted by these "theologies of liberation" as a principle. The conclusion is drawn that the class struggle thus understood divides the church herself, and that in light of this struggle even ecclesial realities must be judged.

The claim is even made that it would maintain an illusion with bad faith to propose that love in its universality can conquer what is the primary structural law of capitalism.

3. According to this conception, the class struggle is the driving force of history. History thus becomes a central notion. It will be affirmed that God himself makes history. It will be added that there is only one history, one in which the distinction between the history of salvation and profane history is no longer necessary. To maintain the distinction would be to fall into "dualism." Affirmations such as these reflect historicist immanentism. Thus there is a tendency to identify the kingdom of God and its growth with the human liberation movement and to make history itself the subject of its own development, as a process of the self-redemption of man by means of the class struggle.

This identification is in opposition to the faith of the church as it has been reaffirmed by the Second Vatican Council.[23]

4. Along these lines, some go so far as to identify God himself with history and to define faith as "fidelity to history," which means adhering to a political policy which is suited to the growth of humanity, conceived of as a purely temporal messianism.

5. As a consequence, faith, hope and charity are given a new content: They become "fidelity to history," "confidence in the future" and "option for the poor." This is tantamount to saying they have been emptied of their theological reality.

6. A radical politicization of faith's affirmations and of theological judgments follows inevitably from this new conception. The question no longer has to do with simply drawing attention to the consequences and political implications of the truths of faith, which are respected beforehand for their transcendent value. In this new system every affirmation of faith or of theology is subordinated to a political criterion which in turn depends on the class struggle, the driving force of history.

7. As a result, participation in the class struggle is presented as a requirement of charity itself. The desire to love everyone here and now, despite his class, and to go out to meet him with the non-violent means of dialogue and persuasion, is denounced as counterproductive and opposed to love.

If one holds that a person should not be the object of hate, it is claimed nevertheless that if he belongs to the objective class of the rich he is primarily a class enemy to be fought. Thus the universality of love of neighbor and brotherhood become an eschatological principle, which will only have meaning for the "new man" who arises out of the victorious revolution.

8. As far as the church is concerned, this system would see her only as a reality interior to history, herself subject to those laws which are supposed to govern the development of history in its immanence. The church, the gift of God and mystery of faith, is emptied of any specific reality by this reductionism. At the same time it is disputed that the participation of Christians who belong to opposing classes at the same eucharistic table still makes any sense.

9. In its positive meaning the "church of the poor" signifies the preference given to the poor, without exclusion, whatever the form of their poverty, because they are preferred by God. The expression also refers to the church of our time, as communion and institution and on the part of her members, becoming more fully conscious of the requirement of evangelical poverty.

10. But the "theologies of liberation," which deserve credit for restoring to a place of honor the great texts of the prophets and of the Gospel in defense of the poor, go on to a disastrous confusion between the poor of the scripture and the proletariat of Marx. In this way they pervert the Christian meaning of the poor, and they transform the fight for the rights of the poor into a class fight within the ideological perspective of the class struggle. For them, the "church of the poor" signifies the church of the class which has become aware of the requirements of the revolutionary struggle as a step toward liberation and which celebrates this liberation in its liturgy.

11. A further remark regarding the expression "church of the people" will not be out of place here. From the pastoral point of view, this expression might mean the favored recipients of evangelization to whom, because of their condition, the church extends her pastoral love first of all. One might also refer to the church as people of God, that is, people of the new covenant established in Christ.[24]

12. But the "theologies of liberation" of which we are speaking mean by church of the people a church of the class, a church of the oppressed people whom it is

necessary to "conscientize" in the light of the organized struggle for freedom. For some, the people, thus understood, even become the object of faith.

13. Building on such a conception of the church of the people, a critique of the very structures of the church is developed. It is not simply the case of fraternal correction of pastors of the church whose behavior does not reflect the evangelical spirit of service and is linked to old-fashioned signs of authority which scandalize the poor. It has to do with a challenge to the sacramental and hierarchical structure of the church, which was willed by the Lord himself. There is a denunciation of members of the hierarchy and the magisterium as objective representatives of the ruling class which has to be opposed. Theologically, this position means that ministers take their origin from the people, who therefore designate ministers of their own choice in accord with the needs of their historic revolutionary mission.

X. A New Hermeneutic

1. The partisan conception of truth, which can be seen in the revolutionary praxis of the class, corroborates this position. Theologians who do not share the theses of the "theology of liberation," the hierarchy and especially the Roman magisterium are thus discredited in advance as belonging to the class of the oppressors. Their theology is a theology of class. Arguments and teachings thus do not have to be examined in themselves since they are only reflections of class interests. Thus the instruction of others is decreed to be, in principle, false.

2. Here is where the global and all-embracing character of the theology of liberation appears. As a result, it must be criticized not just on the basis of this or that affirmation, but on the basis of its classist viewpoint, which it has adopted *a priori* and which has come to function in it as a determining principle.

3. Because of this classist presupposition, it becomes very difficult, not to say impossible, to engage in a real dialogue with some "theologians of liberation" in such a way that the other participant is listened to and his arguments are discussed with objectivity and attention. For these theologians start out with the idea, more or less consciously, that the viewpoint of the oppressed and revolutionary class, which is their own, is the single true point of view. Theological criteria for truth are thus relativized and subordinated to the imperatives of the class struggle. In this perspective, orthodoxy, or the right rule of faith, is substituted by the notion of orthopraxy as the criterion of the truth. In this connection it is important not to confuse practical orientation, which is proper to traditional theology in the same way that speculative orientation is, with the recognized and privileged priority given to a certain type of praxis. For them, this praxis is the revolutionary praxis, which thus becomes the supreme criterion for theological truth. A healthy theological method no doubt will always take the praxis of the church into account and will find there one of its foundations, but that is because that praxis comes from the faith and is a lived expression of it.

4. For the "theologies of liberation" however, the social doctrine of the church is rejected with disdain. It is said that it comes from the illusion of a possible compromise, typical of the middle class, which has no historic destiny.

5. The new hermeneutic inherent in the "theologies of liberation" leads to an essentially political rereading of the scriptures. Thus a major importance is given to the exodus event inasmuch as it is a liberation from political servitude. Likewise, a political reading of the Magnificat is proposed. The mistake here is not in bringing attention to a political dimension of the readings of scripture, but in making of this one dimension the principal or exclusive component. This leads to a reductionist reading of the Bible.

6. Likewise, one places oneself within the perspective of a temporal messianism, which is one of the most radical of the expressions of secularization of the kingdom of God and of its absorption into the immanence of human history.

7. In giving such priority to the political dimension, one is led to deny the radical newness of the New Testament and above all to misunderstand the person of our Lord Jesus Christ, true God and true man, and thus the specific character of the salvation he gave us, that is above all liberation from sin, which is the source of all evils.

8. Moreover in setting aside the authoritative interpretation of the church, denounced as classist, one is at the same time departing from tradition. In that way one is robbed of an essential theological criterion of interpretation and, in the vacuum thus created, one welcomes the most radical theses of rationalist exegesis. Without a critical eye, one returns to the opposition of the "Jesus of history" vs. the "Jesus of faith."

9. Of course the creeds of the faith are literally preserved, especially the Chalcedonian creed, but a new meaning is given to them which is a negation of the faith of the church. On one hand, the Christological doctrine of tradition is rejected in the name of class; on the other hand, one claims to meet again the "Jesus of history" coming from the revolutionary experience of the struggle of the poor for their liberation.

10. One claims to be reliving an experience similar to that of Jesus. The experience of the poor struggling for their liberation, which was Jesus' experience, would thus reveal, and it alone, the knowledge of the true God and of the kingdom.

11. Faith in the incarnate word, dead and risen for all men, and whom "God made Lord and Christ"[25] is denied. In its place is substituted a figure of Jesus who is a kind of symbol who sums up in himself the requirements of the struggle of the oppressed.

12. An exclusively political interpretation is thus given to the death of Christ. In this way its value for salvation and the whole economy of redemption is denied.

13. This new interpretation thus touches the whole of the Christian mystery.

14. In a general way this brings about what can be called an inversion of symbols. Thus instead of seeing, with St. Paul, a figure of baptism in the exodus,[26] some end up making of it a symbol of the political liberation of the people.

15. When the same hermeneutical criterion is applied to the life and to the hierarchical constitution of the church, the relationship between the hierarchy and the "base" becomes the relationship of obedient domination to the law of the struggle of the classes. Sacramentality, which is at the root of the ecclesial ministries and which makes of the church a spiritual reality which cannot be reduced to a purely sociological analysis, is quite simply ignored.

16. This inversion of symbols is likewise verified in the area of the sacraments. The eucharist is no longer to be understood as the real scramental presence of the reconciling sacrifice and as the gift of the body and blood of Christ. It becomes a celebration of the people in their struggle. As a consequence, the unity of the church is radically denied. Unity, reconciliation and communion in love are no longer seen as a gift we receive from Christ.[27] It is the historical class of the poor who by means of their struggle will build unity. For them, the struggle of the classes is the way to unity. The eucharist thus becomes the eucharist of the class. At the same time they deny the triumphant force of the love of God which has been given to us.

XI. Orientations

1. The warning against the serious deviations of some "theologies of liberation" must not at all be taken as some kind of approval, even indirect, of those who keep the poor in misery, who profit from that misery, who notice it while doing nothing about it or who remain indifferent to it. The church, guided by the Gospel of mercy and by the love for mankind, hears the cry for justice[28] and intends to respond to it with all her might.

2. Thus a great call goes out to all the church: With boldness and courage, with farsightedness and prudence, with zeal and strength of spirit, with a love for the poor which demands sacrifice, pastors will consider the response to this call a matter of the highest priority, as many already do.

3. All priests, religious and lay people who hear this call for justice and who want to work for evangelization and the advancement of mankind will do so in communion with their bishop and with the church, each in accord with his or her own specific ecclesial vocation.

4. Aware of the ecclesial character of their vocation, theologians will collaborate loyally and with a spirit of dialogue with the magisterium of the church. They will be able to recognize in the magisterium a gift of Christ to his church[29] and will welcome its word and its directives with filial respect.

5. It is only when one begins with the task of evangelization understood in its entirety that the authentic requirements of human progress and liberation are appreciated. This liberation has as its indispensable pillars: the truth about Jesus the savior, the truth about the church and the truth about man and his dignity.[30]

It is in light of the Beatitudes, and especially the Beatitude of the poor of heart, that the church, which wants to be the church of the poor throughout the world, intends to come to the aid of the noble struggle for truth and justice. She addresses each person, and for that reason, every person. She is the "universal church. The church of the incarnation. She is not the church of one class or another. And she speaks in the name of truth itself. This truth is realistic." It leads to a recognition "of every human reality, every injustice, every tension and every struggle."[31]

6. An effective defense of justice needs to be based on the truth of mankind, created in the image of God and called to the grace of divine sonship. The recognition of the true relationship of human beings to God constitutes the foundation of justice to the extent that it rules the relationships between people. That is why the fight for the rights of man, which the church does not cease to reaffirm, constitutes the authentic fight for justice.

7. The truth of mankind requires that this battle be fought in ways consistent with human dignity. That is why the systematic and deliberate recourse to blind violence, no matter from which side it comes, must be condemned.[32] To put one's trust in violent means in the hope of restoring more justice is to become the victim of a fatal illusion: Violence begets violence and degrades man. It mocks the dignity of man in the person of the victims, and it debases that same dignity among those who practice it.

8. The acute need for radical reforms of the structures which conceal poverty and which are themselves forms of violence should not let us lose sight of the fact that the source of injustice is in the hearts of men. Therefore it is only by making an appeal to the moral potential of the person and to the constant need for interior conversion that social change will be brought about which will truly be in the service of man.[33] For it will only be in the measure that they collaborate freely in these necessary changes through their own initiative and in solidarity, that people, awakened to a sense of their responsibility, will grow in humanity.

The inversion of morality and structures is steeped in a materialist anthropology which is incompatible with the dignity of mankind.

9. It is therefore an equally fatal illusion to believe that these new structures will of themselves give birth to a "new man" in the sense of the truth of man. The Christian cannot forget that it is only the Holy Spirit, who has been given to us, who is the source of every true renewal and that God is the Lord of history.

10. By the same token, the overthrow by means of revolutionary violence of structures which generate violence is not *ipso facto* the beginning of a just regime. A major fact of our time ought to evoke the reflection of all those who would sincerely work for the true liberation of their brothers: Millions of our own contemporaries legitimately yearn to recover those basic freedoms of which they were deprived by totalitarian and atheistic regimes which came to power by violent and revolutionary means, precisely in the name of the liberation of the people. This shame of our time cannot be ignored: While claiming to bring them freedom, these regimes keep whole nations in conditions of servitude which are unworthy of mankind. Those who, perhaps inadvertently, make themselves accomplices of similar enslavements betray the very poor they mean to help.

11. The class struggle as a road toward a classless society is a myth which slows reform and aggravates poverty and injustice. Those who allow themselves to be caught up in fascination with this myth should reflect on the bitter examples history has to offer about where it leads. They would then understand that we are not talking here about abandoning an effective means of struggle on behalf of the poor for an ideal which has no practical effects. On the contrary, we are talking about freeing oneself from a delusion in order to base oneself squarely on the Gospel and its power of realization.

12. One of the conditions for necessary theological correction is giving proper value to the social teaching of the church. This teaching is by no means closed. It is, on the contrary, open to all the new questions which are so numerous today. In this perspective, the contribution of theologians and other thinkers in all parts of the world to the reflection of the church is indispensable today.

13. Likewise the experience of those who work directly for evangelization and for the advancement of the poor and the oppressed is necessary for the doctrinal and pastoral reflection of the church. In this sense it is necessary to affirm that one becomes more aware of certain aspects of truth by starting with praxis, if by that one means pastoral praxis and social work which keeps its evangelical inspiration.

14. The teaching of the church on social issues indicates the main lines of ethical orientation. But in order that it be able to guide action directly, the church needs competent people from a scientific and technological viewpoint, as well as in the human and political sciences. Pastors should be attentive to the formation of persons of such capability who live the Gospel deeply. Lay persons, whose proper mission is to build society, are involved here to the highest degree.

15. Theses of the "theologies of liberation" are widely popularized under a simplified form in formation sessions or in what are called "base groups" which lack the necessary catechetical and theological preparation as well as the capacity for discernment. Thus these theses are accepted by generous men and women without any critical judgment being made.

16. That is why pastors must look after the quality and the content of catechesis and formation, which should always present the whole message of salvation and the imperatives of true liberation within the framework of this whole message.

17. In this full presentation of Christianity, it is proper to emphasize those essential aspects which the "theologies of liberation" especially tend to misunderstand or to eliminate, namely: the transcendence and gratuity of liberation in Jesus Christ, true God and true man; the sovereignty of grace; and the true nature of the means of salvation, especially of the church and the sacraments. One should also keep in mind the true meaning of ethics, in which the distinction between good and evil is not relativized, the real meaning of sin, the necessity for conversion and the universality of the law of fraternal love.

One needs to be on guard against the politicization of existence, which, misunderstanding the entire meaning of the kingdom of God and the transcendence of the person, begins to sacralize politics and betray the religion of the people in favor of the projects of the revolution.

18. The defenders of orthodoxy are sometimes accused of passivity, indulgence or culpable complicity regarding the intolerable situations of injustice and the political regimes which prolong them. Spiritual conversion, the intensity of the love of God and neighbor, zeal for justice and peace, the gospel meaning of the poor and of poverty, are required of everyone and especially of pastors and those in positions of responsibility. The concern for the purity of the faith demands giving the answer of effective witness in the service of one's neighbor, the poor and the oppressed in particular, in an integral theological fashion. By the witness of their dynamic and constructive power to love, Christians will thus lay the foundations of this "civilization of love" of which the conference of Puebla spoke, following Paul VI.[34] Moreover there are already many priests, religious and lay people who are consecrated in a truly evangelical way for the creation of a just society.

Conclusion

The words of Paul VI in his "Profession of Faith," express with full clarity the faith of the church, from which one cannot deviate without provoking, besides spiritual disaster, new miseries and new types of slavery.

"We profess our faith that the kingdom of God, begun here below in the church of Christ, is not of this world, whose form is passing away, and that its own growth cannot be confused with the progress of civilization, of science, of human technology, but that it consists in knowing ever more deeply the unfathomable riches of Christ, to hope ever more strongly in things eternal, to respond ever more ardently to the love of God, to spread ever more widely grace and holiness among men. But it is this very same love which makes the church constantly concerned for the true temporal good of mankind as well. Never ceasing to recall to her children that they have no lasting dwelling here on earth, she urges them also to contribute, each according to his own vocation and means, to the welfare of their earthly city, to promote justice, peace and brotherhood among men, to lavish their assistance on their brothers, especially on the poor and the most dispirited. The intense concern of the church, the bride of Christ, for the needs of mankind, their joys and their hopes, their pains and their struggles, is nothing other than the great desire to be present to them in order to enlighten them with the light of Christ and join them all to him, their only Savior. It can never mean that the church is conforming to the things of this world nor that she is lessening the earnestness with which she awaits her Lord and the eternal kingdom."[35]

This instruction was adopted at an ordinary meeting of the Sacred Congregation for the Doctrine of the Faith and was approved at an audience granted to the undersigned cardinal prefect by His Holiness Pope John Paul II, who ordered its publication.

Given at Rome, at the Sacred Congregation for the Doctrine of the Faith, Aug. 6, 1984, the feast of the Transfiguration of Our Lord.

Cardinal Joseph Ratzinger   Archbishop Alberto Bovone
Prefect   Secretary

NOTES

1. Cf. *Gaudium et Spes*, 4.
2. Cf. *Dei Verbum*, 10.
3. Cf. Gal. 5:1ff.
4. Cf. Ex. 24.
5. Cf. Jer. 31:31–34; Ez. 38:26ff.
6. Cf. Zec. 3:12ff.
7. Cf. Dt. 10:18–19.
8. Cf. Lk. 10:25–37.
9. Cf. 2 Cor. 8:9.
10. Cf. Mt. 25:31–46; Acts 9:4-5; Col. 1:24.
11. Cf. Jas. 5ff.
12. Cf. 1 Cor. 11:17–34.
13. Cf. Jas. 2:14–26.
14. Cf. Acta Apostolicae Sedis 71 (1979) pp. 1144–1160.
15. Cf. AAS 71 (1979) p. 196.
16. Cf. *Evangelii Nuntiandi*, 25–33, AAS 68 (1976) pp. 23-28.
17. Cf. *Evangelii Nuntiandi*, 32, AAS 68 (1976) p. 27.
18. Cf. AAS 71 (1979) pp. 188–196.
19. Cf. *Gaudium et Spes*, 39; Pius XI, *Quadragesimo Anno:* AAS 23 (1931) p. 207.
20. Cf. nos. 1134-1165 and nos. 1166–1205.
21. Cf. Puebla Document, IV, 2.
22. Cf. Paul VI, *Octogesima Adveniens*, 34, AAS 63 (1971) pp. 424–425.
23. Cf. *Lumen Gentium*, 9–17.
24. Cf. *Gaudium et Spes*, 39.
25. Cf. Acts 2:36.
26. Cf. 1 Cor. 10:1-2.
27. Cf. Eph. 2:11-22.
28. Cf. Puebla Document I, II, 3.3.
29. Cf. Lk. 10:16.
30. Cf. John Paul II, Address at the Opening of the Conference at Puebla, AAS 71 (1979) pp. 188–196; Puebla Document, II P, c.1.
31. Cf. John Paul II, Address to the Favela Vidigal at Rio de Janeiro, July 2, 1980, AAS 72 (1980) pp. 852-858.
32. Cf. Puebla Document, II, c. II, 5.4.
33. Cf. *ibid.,* IV. c.3. 3.1.
34. Cf. *ibid.,* IV, II, 2.3.
35. Cf. Paul VI, Profession of Faith of the People of God, June 30, 1968, AAS 60, (1968) pp. 443–444.